Client/Server

BCS Practitioner Series

Series editor: Ray Welland

Client/Server

A handbook of modern computer system design

The

Client Server Group
of the British Computer Society

Clive Evans
David Lacey
David Harvey
David Gibbons
&
Andy Krasun

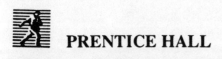

PRENTICE HALL

LONDON • NEW YORK • TORONTO • SYDNEY • TOKYO • SINGAPORE • MADRID • MEXICO CITY • MUNICH

First published 1995 by
Prentice Hall International (UK) Ltd
Campus 400, Maylands Avenue
Hemel Hempstead
Hertfordshire, HP2 7EZ
A division of
Simon & Schuster International Group

Typeset in 10/12 pt Times
by Photoprint, Torquay, Devon

Printed and bound in Great Britain by
T.J. Press (Padstow) Ltd, Padstow, Cornwall.

Library of Congress Cataloging-in-Publication Data

Client/server: a handbook of modern computer
system design / by Clive Evans . . . [et al.].
        p. cm. -- (The BCS practitioner series)
        Includes bibliographical references and index.
        ISBN 0–13–377201–2
        1. Client/server computing. 2. System design--
Handbooks, manuals, etc. I. Evans, Clive.
II. Series.
    QA76.9.C55C54   1995
    004'.36--dc20   95–14232
                                         CIP

British Library Cataloguing in Publication Data

A catalogue record for this book is available from
the British Library

ISBN 0–13–377201–2

1 2 3 4 5   99 98 97 96 95

Contents

Foreword

When Clive first approached me with an idea for a working group on the architecture of client server systems, my initial reaction was to say 'of course. . .' – like all good ideas the only amazing thing about it was that nobody had done it before. Later when he had put together the group it was obvious that there was lots of interest in their work and a significant need for the results. In fact my only feeling of unease concerned the name of the group – LEGHAWK. It was (to put it nicely) less than snappy and not in keeping with most names throughout the computer industry (i.e., either a meaningless three letter acronym or an obscure name from Roman or Greek mythology).

However, I am glad to say that the whole thing worked out well – the name has grown on us (although it still isn't very snappy) and the work carried out by the group has resulted in a very good and useable book.

In fact, it is probably no exaggeration to say that this book addresses one of the key problems facing designers of client server systems today – how to describe a distributed system. One of the problems with client server is that the systems it includes can differ widely – from simple database server based architectures to complex real-time application server based systems. As Clive realised, we need to describe each system using a standard notation.

It is true to say that only when you can describe such systems can you compare them, measure them, define generic architectures for them and identify methods for building them.

This book describes such a notation. For that reason alone, I consider it one of the most important books on the subject to be written in 1995.

Nick Evans
London 1995

Editorial preface

The widespread use of PCs in business has caused a major re-think of systems architectures. Client/server architectures, with powerful clients, are replacing the traditional centralised systems with dumb terminals. This book discusses the technical aspects of client/server architectures and, equally importantly, it covers topics such as system management implications and costs. The migration from legacy systems to client/server architectures is a major problem and this book includes discussion of migration issues and a case study to show that it can be done. This book grew out of the work of the Client/Server Specialist Group of the BCS and contains much valuable advice for practitioners.

Ray Welland

Preface

This book is in three sections. In the first section (Chapters 1 to 6) we cover the main areas of concern in the design of client/server systems, including, in Chapter 5, a framework for a gradual shift from legacy to client/server systems. Next, there are two case studies. The first describes how such a migration to client/server is being accomplished. The second is a description of how a client/server architecture was implemented.

The two appendices cover topics that we feel are useful adjuncts to a knowledge of client/server design. First, the LEGHAWK notation, which is used throughout the book, is expanded. The second appendix describes transaction processing systems, and the services they provide.

Chapter 1, Overview of Client/server Systems, introduces the concepts of client/server, and some of its benefits. Then we consider aspects of the design concerning specifications and service levels, user interfaces, data distribution, and the distribution of processing power. Here we stress that client/server design is more driven by the users than previous architectures.

In Chapter 2, Systems Management, those aspects specific to client/server are discussed. These include user support, change management, availability, security, asset management, and aspects of capacity planning and performance management are also discussed.

Chapter 3, System Design, identifies different categories of client/server architecture, and explains the major differences between the two major types, MIS and OLTP. We consider the advantages of layering the components, and the impact of the choice of platform, the user interface, the network, the database, and the implications of printing requirements. Under application design, the emphasis is on OLTP, and we consider the implications of different transaction cycle and data locking strategies. The advantages of context-free servers are explained, and also the potential of the parallel use of client and server processors. We consider the implications of using servers as clients, and offer some tips for producing robust application servers.

Chapter 4, Connectivity, discusses various mechanisms for joining the components of a client/server system, and their impact on network traffic. The three types of Middleware – Distributed Computing, Database Access and OLTP Monitors – are explained. A final section describes communications techniques for OLTP systems in some detail.

In Chapter 5, Migration and Coexistence, the gradual incorporation of client/server into an existing computing environment is discussed in detail. This process is presented as a phased approach. Strategies for coexistence of legacy and client/server systems are presented. A final section deals with the impact such a change of approach has on users, managers and IT personnel.

Chapter 6, Costs, discusses the financial implications of introducing client/server systems and identifies areas of cost – especially long-term cost – that are sometimes forgotten or ignored.

Then follow two case studies.

In Chapter 7, Migration Case Study, Air Products explain how they migrated to a client/server architecture. They describe their criteria for the new system, and their choice of software and hardware components. The main issues that emerge are the need for learning new programming skills (the transition from procedural code to event-driven programming), and the management of the way change impacts on people.

Chapter 8, Case Study: the Prefix Architecture, discusses, in some technical depth, the inner workings of a particular OLTP client/server architecture, illustrating the types of problems that such an architecture has to resolve.

Chapter 9 is a summary of the main points of the book, together with a hesitant peep at the future.

In Appendix 1, LEGHAWK, we explain the principles of the notation (which is used extensively throughout the book), and describe its use. The notation is applied to the Prefix architecture as an example.

Appendix 2, Transaction Processing Systems, provides an overview of the principles of transaction processing systems, and describes how they can transparently provide services to application programmers and system designers.

The Glossary is where you discover what all the TLAs (Three Letter Acronyms) really mean. It is an essential guide to the jargon-prone world of modern computing.

Acknowledgements

'This is dedicated to the one I love' – Mommas and Poppas.

This book sprang from the collective loins of a working party set up under the auspices of the Client/Server Group of the British Computer Society by the present chairman, Nick Evans. The remit of the working party was to come up with some classification of client/server systems, and some guidelines as to the attributes of the different classes.

The authors are all original members of that working party, but two others found the process of writing a book more than they could bear. Victor Wu fled to Hong Kong, Jose Arraujo didn't. They don't get their names on the authors list, but we do owe them a great deal for their contribution to our discussions, and for the use of their initials in the LEGHAWK name (qv).

Thanks are also due to Viki Williams of Prentice Hall for bubbling with enthusiasm for the book at a time when the authors were still struggling, but progress had ceased. Without that injection of enthusiasm, we might have given up – and what a loss that would have been.

Finally, we owe a vote of thanks to our respective companies for supporting us in this endeavour, but it has to be said that the book represents the views of the authors, rather than those of nCube, AT&T, EDS, IBM, Iridium or Air Products. Particular thanks go to colleagues at AT&T GIS (UK) for reviewing the book, and making encouraging noises and constructive comments.

About the authors

The chairman of the working party, and the overall editor of the book, is Clive Evans (MA, MBCS, CEng) who is a Systems Engineering Manager with nCube. He spent his formative years (all 23 of them) in Systems Engineering with IBM, leaving to join Teradata, famous for its parallel relational database engine.

David Lacey (BSc, Sydney and London, MBCS), who first had the idea for the LEGHAWK notation, is a founder member of Iridium, a firm of IT Consulting Engineers. He has worked for the Real Time Special Interest Group in Boston specifying extensions to UNIX for real-time processing. Latterly, he has developed a client/server architecture for a London-based financial software house.

David Gibbons (MBCS) works for Air Products in Surrey. He has been closely involved in developing and implementing their strategy to move away from a mini/mainframe environment to a true client/server architecture. His other main responsibility is to assist programming teams implement the disciplines of Total Quality Management.

David Harvey (BSc, MSc, MBCS, CEng, Eur Ing) works for EDS (formerly Scicon). He is currently project manager for their Work Management System, a client/server system designed for the engineering department of a large multinational oil company. He has installed systems in some pretty unlikely places.

Andy Krasun (BA, MSc, MBCS, CEng) has worked for IBM since the dawn of time. He is currently working on CICS for OS/2, but has worked on CICS since responsibility for it came to England in 1975. His latest triumph was providing consultation to the administrative systems for the Winter Olympics in Lillehammer.

Introduction

'Client/server' computing has turned much of the established thinking about computer systems on its head – or rather it has turned it right side up, in that it puts the client first and then defines the services to be provided. In the past, the demands of the computer system have tended to dominate the needs of the user. The state of technology has largely been to blame for this – computers have traditionally been expensive and difficult, and therefore centralized and surrounded by specialists. With the arrival of the cheap, powerful PC which is approachable by the average human being, and will not only do serious and useful things such as word processing, but also play games, a new approach to computer systems has also arrived.

The term 'client/server' qualifies as a 'porridge' word, defined by Edward de Bono as a word whose meaning is not clearly defined, but which nevertheless represents an important idea. The danger is, of course, that porridge words get to mean different things to different people, and that is surely true of 'client/server'. We will provide a formal definition later, but informally it embraces the notion of a computer system made up exclusively of a set of 'servers' and a set of 'clients'. Each server provides a well-defined service, each client can have access to one or more services. Clients and servers communicate through well-defined interfaces, typically over telecommunications links, of which the favourite is the local area network (LAN). The client is usually thought of as a workstation, by which we mean a device similar to a PC.

The notion of 'client/server' came into being as a direct result of the arrival of PCs and LANs, and is in contrast to the world of mainframes, surrounded by their slavish terminals. Indeed, one use of the term 'client/server' is to describe a world as far removed from mainframes as possible, although in truth, mainframes can be used as servers. What is currently deemed 'bad' about mainframes is their unfriendliness, their complexity, their cost, their slowness to respond, and what is wonderful about PCs is that they are the reverse. Personal computers, however, suffer precisely from being personal, that is, they do not provide access to central facilities. Local area networks solve that problem, allowing PCs to blossom into workstations, which may have access to services of all kinds. In general, the most important services are those which provide access to data.

'Client/server' is also a new way of thinking about computers, and one which holds out the promise of systems that are genuinely engineered in the way that other constructs are engineered, such as bridges, or buildings, or ships. Architects design according to well-understood rules, and use reference books to help select materials and components. If computer systems were constructed from special-purpose servers, client workstations and telecommunication networks, each of these components could be precisely defined, and acquired, as in any other discipline. Furthermore, market forces could operate to stimulate the production of a range of servers, from the cheap and cheerful to the sophisticated and expensive, for everything from fax transmission to relational database management, allowing customers a control over their computing costs that they have not enjoyed to date.

In this book we introduce a notation – LEGHAWK – which allows client/server systems to be accurately and concisely documented. Each level of a system is broken down into its component parts: the presentation component (represented by the letter P), application or business logic component (A), the database (D), the routing mechanism (R), and the communications links ($\sim$C$\sim$) between them. Their grouping onto computing platforms are also represented using the symbol [], and their attributes may be described to whatever level is deemed appropriate. We believe that such a notation will improve design generally by providing a means to document a system thoroughly and consistently. It may help bring computer systems design more into line with other engineering design disciplines.

The notation also emphasizes the building blocks that are used in this book: we do not address the niceties of database design in any detail except where that differs for client/server systems. The same is true of interface design and telecommunications – this is not a book about those specialist subjects, it is about how to combine them into working systems.

Perhaps more important than all of this is that 'client/server' systems are entirely understandable by ordinary human beings, such as senior executives and junior managers. Much of the mystique and fear of computers may be blown away, making them as much part of everyday life as are the electrical sockets in the wall, and as susceptible to normal management disciplines. Computers are too important to be left to specialists.

This book is written as a genuine handbook for use by professionals when designing computer systems, but also in the hope that people other than computer specialists will read most of it and find it approachable.

1 Overview of client/server systems

We had better begin with a definition of client/server systems. These are systems which may be decomposed into three elements: servers, clients, and the links between them. A server provides a clearly defined set of services, and a documented interface for activating those services. A client requests services, processes the results and presents them. The linkage between a client and its servers may be based on telecommunication links between processors or may be a simple call within the same processor. A server may also act as a client, calling on further servers.

In practice, a computer system usually has client/server components within it rather than being 'client/server' at every level and in every aspect. Indeed, even the disreputable mainframe can claim some aspects of client/server: the operating system has many of the characteristics of a server.

There is also a strong link between a server and a collection of 'objects'. In object-oriented thinking the world is created from objects, which, exactly like servers, have a well-defined purpose, and are activated by a well-defined interface, using, in this case, a message mechanism. Any object-oriented system is almost bound to result in a 'client/server' design.

There is also a clear relationship with open systems: if the interfaces used within a client/server system adhere to international standards, then it is an open system. Again, very few systems are completely open – if only because the definitions are far from complete – they usually exploit some standards in some areas (SQL, for example).

Finally, there is a tendency for client/server systems to be distributed: however, this is far from being a rule. Most systems require many servers to meet the needs of its users, and the initial design will no doubt document them as separate entities. But there are many grounds on which to combine those services onto a small number of platforms, as we shall see later. The ability to provide a wide range of services is one of the strengths of the mainframe as a server platform.

The most common implementation of client/server design is the PC-style workstation connected over LAN and WAN to servers located either at local or central levels or at both. Such systems are increasingly used to provide a wide range of services to users, who are thus empowered to handle a large number of tasks within the organization.

Typical servers include electronic mail, relational databases, print and fax, and workflow. Typical clients are based on Microsoft Windows with a variety of tools such as spreadsheets, word processors, and SQL access mechanisms. A user thus equipped is in a position to enquire on central company data, download it into local facilities, manipulate and display it, include it in documents, and transmit the results both within and outside the organization.

A given hardware platform may provide both client and server functionality: in particular, most platforms will provide not only their business function but also a system management function. Thus a workstation clearly provides client functionality via its presentation (P) capabilities, but may also supply services at the request of the central system management client. Let us summarize the benefits of designing systems in 'client/server' style.

1. *Platform cost.* An important feature of servers is that they provide a defined set of services through a well-defined interface. This means that real competition can emerge to drive down prices. This is especially true in today's environment where the price of the basic technology continues to fall apace. A good example is the database server, an almost universal requirement in a computer system. There are several reputable suppliers of relational database systems in the market, each providing a similar set of base functions, supplemented by tempting extras such as toolsets, SQL extensions, and ready-made packages. The designer thus has a choice among these products. Furthermore, there is a race among hardware suppliers to produce systems that will run these products faster and more cost-effectively than their competitors. So the designer also has a choice of hardware platforms. The TPC benchmarks are an example of this process at work. Client/server computing in particular, and open computing in general, breaks down computer systems into modular components, in each of which market forces can operate to reduce prices.

2. *Clarity of description.* Client/server systems are readily described as a series of components, linked through clear interfaces. Each component has a well-defined task to perform. By contrast, centralized systems perform every task on the same platform − from user interaction to telecommunications to database searching. This makes the platform a very complicated place indeed. Clarity and simplicity in design is one of the goals that links engineers of every kind.

3. *Graphical user interfaces.* The staggering capabilities of the PC in handling graphics can completely transform the way in which the humble human being can communicate with the mighty computer. The spreadsheet is the most obvious example of an exploitation of this capability which has allowed millions of people to make use of computers in an intuitive way. Link the spreadsheet on the desktop to

the database at head office, and you have delivered a very powerful tool for helping to run even the largest businesses.

4. *Speed of implementation*. Client/server systems operate on the basis of tools placed in the hands of users, rather than systems specified and built by computer professionals. This means that a user has much more control over his or her own computing destiny – certainly changes in presentation formats can be handled directly by the user. Tools such as spreadsheets and word processors can be purchased 'off the shelf'. The behaviour of servers can be extended by changing parameters rather than by adding new code.

    Increasingly, we can expect users to respond to changes dynamically, rather than waiting for systems people to attend to their needs. The role of the systems people will be to react to changed usage of the servers, in much the same way as an electricity provider monitors usage, and switches in additional resources to meet the demands of the Christmas turkey.

    There is, of course, an implication that the user knows how to use the tools – we will return to this point later.

5. *Quality*. Building a system from special-purpose components, such as a database server, local area network and workstation, each of which is used by many other organizations around the world, is more likely to be robust and reliable than a system which is built from scratch. Each component should operate at very high levels of availability – provided it is working within its limitations – and deliver a very robust system. A 'hand-built' system is almost expected to include errors.

6. *Expandability*. Adding new facilities to a 'client/server' system can be as easy as adding a new server into the network, and enabling access from the existing workstations. The possibilities are endless already, and increasing steadily. External facilities can also be exploited with relative ease: a service such as Compuserve might prove to be the quickest way to provide an electronic mail system without writing a line of code. Centralized systems are necessarily limited by what can be run on the central system.

Perhaps most importantly, such systems are in tune with current thinking about empowering the workforce and slimming management structures. There is no doubt that client/server systems are able to put an immense amount of function at the fingertips of suitably trained individuals, allowing them to handle a great range of tasks or to deal with issues which previously called upon a whole department to analyse data. Client/server systems can help harness the immense capabilities of the computer to the successful running of businesses, with the minimum of administrative overheads and the maximum responsiveness to competitive demands. Businesses may look to client/server technology to provide:

- A repository for data from a variety of systems
- A coherent user interface to a variety of systems
- Swift application development
- Better value from PCs already installed

The reality of 'client/server' systems is, of course, that while we can certainly see that the benefits outlined are there for the taking, their implementation can be difficult. There are new problems inherent in this style of design, and some new costs, too, which are often being discovered 'the hard way'. Such successful systems as there are tend to be on a small scale, either implemented round a single LAN or within a department with special needs within a large organization.

There is also the problem of migration from existing 'legacy' systems to be faced, a topic which we address in a later chapter. Our purpose in this book is to enable the benefits while avoiding the pitfalls, to provide a balanced view to help a systems designer to choose the optimum system to meet a given requirement.

An overview of design considerations

For any given requirement, there are many ways to design a viable computer system. All of them will work, but they will have different attributes and costs. Cost is a subject that we will consider separately, because cost is not only very important it is also much more complicated than it might seem. The user interface can range between a multimedia production and a blank screen, the data and the application function may be distributed or centralized, it may be open or proprietary.

The system specification

In the bad old days – which are still with us in some quarters – IT specialists would descend on a department that wanted a system and analyze it. They would write a detailed specification – often running to hundreds of pages – demand a signature from the harassed manager, then disappear for three years. On their return, they would deliver the system as specified and be mortified to learn that it wasn't at all what the user really wanted.

This description – while somewhat tongue in cheek – is not far from reality. IT departments felt that they had to specify requirements in great detail to protect themselves from the alternative phenomenon – that of user departments changing requirements during the building of the system. Such changes would inevitably have technical repercussions beyond the understanding of the users, and lead to accumulating delays.

At the root of the problem, of course, lay the time taken to conceive and build a system – client/server technology can help here by using larger building blocks. It can also help by using PC tools to build a prototype of the system very quickly, perhaps as part of the system specification.

It is still important to have a system specification, but it should not be so detailed that it is never read at all. It should contain a description of the business use that is intended, the major facilities required, who the users will be, and what service levels are required. This last point is most important, and frequently overlooked – the service levels needed can make a huge difference to the cost of a system. A system that must genuinely be available 24 hours per day, every day (such as a worldwide airline reservations system) will need a great deal of attention paid to system management issues, and almost certainly require replicated systems to handle failures.

Agreeing these service levels is an important part of the design process, and is not always easy to do. Everyone believes that their system is vital, but in fact, most systems can afford to be 'down' for some period with only a minor impact on the business. The systems classed as 'Management Information Systems' usually fall into this bracket – they are crucial to the planning of the business, but not to its day-to-day operation. If they are not available for an hour, the business will likely survive.

There is, however, a creeping dependency on such systems. When first installed, managers may agree that they can indeed live for an hour without the system. But as time goes by, and the system becomes part of the fabric of everyday life, it is expected to be available, no matter the negotiated agreement. It is better to be able to go back and renegotiate the service level, and agree the extra cost of complete reliability, so the inclusion of service levels is important.

Similarly, it is important to include expected data sizes and user populations in the specification, because these also suffer from creeping increases: more and more people may demand access to the system, and more and more data may be added to the databases. Sooner or later, response and processing times will reveal that the system is overloaded and needs upgrading. Again it is important to be able to go back to the original specifications to understand that the growth is genuinely outside what was originally envisaged.

These parameters are not specified simply to 'cover the designer's behind' when the system begins to behave abnormally – although there is just an element of that – it is primarily to ensure that the computer system is run in an orderly and managed fashion, that growth is accounted for, and new levels of performance costed and agreed.

The users

The most important element in any system design is its user population. This is not mere servility to those who foot the bill, but a reflection of the fact that most other aspects of the system are predictable and malleable: people often surprise you. It must also be borne in mind that ordinary users are not as system designers are: system designers are usually computer people, who enjoy making their workstations play 'Its a Hap hap happy day' when powered on. Ordinary people are not like that. They are more likely afraid of computers, and will certainly have strong views about what constitutes 'user-friendliness'.

It is most important to understand those users, what part the system will play in their lives, and what other systems they already use. This will help to determine the interface to be provided, and the training costs. It may well alter the design of the whole system. In one insurance company that was considering the implementation of a graphical interface, the designer spent a day with the users, and discovered that – far from the system being an important part of the departments work, which is what the IT department felt – it was the provider of a relatively minor part of the information they needed during the day. They actually spent more time looking up data in tables of printed information, retrieving letters, and answering the phone than ever they did using the existing computer system. So to put a smart new front-end on it would not change their lives – certainly not their productivity – unless these other sources of information were provided in the same way.

The most valuable computer systems actually change the way that jobs are done, rather than just automating them (re-engineering is the received terminology). This means changing how the user spends his or her day, and that level of change is often uncomfortable. It is a responsibility of the system designer to ensure that the users will be ready to accept this change, which means planning training carefully, but also involving users in the design and evaluation process. What they perceive as 'user-friendly' is an important factor.

By way of example, a document distribution system was to be installed in the offices of a large manufacturing organization to provide a swift exchange mechanism between the office of the Group Chief Executive and those of the divisional Chief Executives. The most important user was thus the secretary to the Group Chief Executive, and she was a lady with clear views. Although the plan was to deliver documents electronically – at the touch of a function key – without any paper being involved, she was not comfortable with the technology, preferring to print the documents and fax them individually. No amount of selling the benefits would change her: she just didn't see it through the eyes of a system designer.

It is important not to forget secondary users of the system, or those who will be directly impacted by it. Most systems are not restricted to users sitting at screens. For example, if a large overnight print run is envisaged, to produce the day's invoices, the designer had better consult the print room about getting the invoices into envelopes and into the hands of the Post Office.

The user interface

Closely allied with the users are their interfaces to the system, and the whole business of 'user-friendliness'. Much is written on the subject of graphical user interfaces (GUI) versus character-based interfaces (pictures versus letters) often with deeply felt emotion. The fact is that the human animal is actually quite adept at learning interfaces if properly motivated so to do. Examine a knitting pattern if you will – mere gobbledegook to all but millions of ordinary knitters who can glance at pages of the stuff and generate ill-fitting Christmas presents. Consider the motor car, which involves the use of most parts of the body in synchronized combinations, and ask yourself whether that same person could push a mouse around a mat.

The choice of interface is important but not crucial. People can and will adapt to the craziest interfaces if they have to – such as the QWERTY keyboard – and even get to like them. The interface has at least to allow people to do something that they want or need to do, and should get in the way as little as possible. Ideally, it should be helpful, intuitive, encouraging, and adaptive.

One important subsidiary decision is whether a graphical interface should be used or not. Character-based interfaces can run on cheap terminals, and are perfectly satisfactory for simple, repetitive tasks. The most obvious example of this may be seen in data-entry departments. Your serious data-entry clerk looks at the document to be transcribed, and not at the screen unless it squawks. There is no point in spending hundreds of pounds on a screen that will never be viewed.

If a graphical user interface *is* chosen, and if this is the first time that many users have seen such a thing, then training is essential. Such interfaces have great merits once the basics are well understood by the users. There is a good analogy with driving a car. Once the techniques have been mastered, one may drive almost any car in the world, but mastering those techniques is not a trivial task.

Graphical user interfaces come into their own when a large variety of different facilities are available through the same workstation – which is the vision behind client/server systems. The workstation is an important element in fusing these differing services together in a seamless fashion using facilities such as OLE or DDE. The object/action paradigm does seem to offer an intuitive way of presenting system-based facilities to the human being. This presents facilities to the user in the form of recognizable objects (icons) with a range of 'actions' presented separately. The user first selects an object (such as a document), and then decides what action to undertake (such as editing or mailing it).

The workstation also has an important role to play in adapting computer systems for use by people with disabilities – severe or minor. Millions of people suffer from partial colour blindness, for example, and the use of PC technology to provide interfaces to severely disabled people is well known.

Client/server systems tend to be associated automatically with graphical user interfaces, but this is far from correct. A simple terminal connected to a local terminal server which in turn requests services from other servers is a fine, upstanding example of client/server technology.

Data

It is the processing of data that gives the entire industry its name, but its the storage and maintenance of data – rather than the processing – that's at the heart of a designer's problems. After understanding the users, planning the location and management of the data is the most important feature of a design. And it's more difficult in a client/server environment than in a traditional system. In a world consisting solely of central processors and 'dumb' terminals, the data can only reside in one place. In a world of powerful workstations and distributed servers, data may reside at a variety of places.

In the case of a large organization we may expect to find servers in local offices, regional offices, and corporate offices and to find workstations with significant data storage capabilities. For each piece of data there is a natural audience of potential users, and generally that audience determines the lowest point at which data may sensibly be stored. If the audience is contained within a department, then the departmental server is an obvious candidate for the storage of that data. However, there is always the option of providing the data storage at a higher level in the hierarchy and supplying telecommunications links to it. There is rarely a case for storing it at a lower level, and almost none for storing anything other than temporary data on the workstation itself. The reasons for this are availability and security: workstations are very likely to be switched off when the user goes home, thus denying access to others. Equally, the workstation is exposed to tampering and outright theft, as in the case of the portable PC containing plans for the Gulf War, stolen from the back of a car.

What we are discussing here is also to do with the argument of 'centralized versus distributed' databases. Some pundits believe that distributing data around departmental servers is the right approach, others argue that keeping data centrally provides better all-round access combined with security. There is no right answer, the location of data is merely one of the important decisions that a systems designer must make.

Allied to this decision is one about how much copying of data there is to be: it is vital that a designer keeps in mind where the prime copy of data is kept, so that its integrity may be safeguarded. However, there will often be cases where the provision of a copy of the data is the optimum mechanism for providing access. This is particularly true where the data need not be completely up-to-date, as with many marketing and management requirements, where information as of yesterday is perfectly adequate for their needs.

Copying data is, of course, a potential headache, and there must be a proper mechanism for ensuring that copies are indeed provided either regularly or as required. In fact, both kinds of provision are often needed, with regular copies being supplemented by occasional special requests.

A fashionable – and useful – concept is that of the data warehouse, which as its name implies, is a central repository of a wide range of data, to meet the needs of a wide range of users. It is typical of a commercial organization that there are a number of departments associated with the day-to-day running of the business, and these departments generate data on their respective computer systems. A great raft of other departments whose job is to support and manage those day-to-day operations need access to that data. The data warehouse is one way of meeting their needs, which are typically unpredictable and especially unsuited to the rigorous methods of analysis which we were gently mocking earlier in this chapter.

The data warehouse is one of the simplest ways of introducing client/ server technology to an existing organization, which already has its operational systems in place, gathering data. Providing access to that data and a tool set on a powerful workstation to process it can quickly provide real value to an organization. We will return to data and its handling later in this book.

Processing

As with data, processing may also be distributed these days. Indeed, 'client/server' design implies that serious thought has gone into the location of application logic. Again, this is more difficult than with traditional design, where all aspects of the application ran on the central processor – end of debate.

That part of processing which is associated with the presentation of data, or of navigation options, is the most natural part to migrate to the local workstation. This is, of course, because the workstation can provide fast response to trivial requests, and a highly sophisticated graphical interface, if required. In order to maximize the impact of such an interface, however, some aspects of the application will need to migrate down to the workstation too. An obvious example of this are the lists of possibilities for selection by a user. The idea of selecting from a list of possibilities, rather than simply typing in an entry, is a powerful aid to increasing the accuracy of users.

By way of example, consider a user who has to enter information about the sort of bank account a customer wishes to open. The choice is between cheque, savings, deposit, money market and so on. This list is variable: new account types may be added. So if this list is actually stored on the workstation, it will need to be updated as necessary – and a mechanism must be built to transmit the new list to every workstation. If it is stored centrally, response times will suffer – and the whole point of graphical user interfaces is that they should be responsive. It is another choice for the designer.

One important decision for the designer is whether or not to use a transaction processing monitor as part of the system: some vendors of databases and tool sets would claim that such a thing is only an extra complication. We shall discuss this issue in later chapters.

In most commercial applications the amount of processing per transaction is really quite small. Arithmetic extends not much further than adding lists of numbers, adding percentages for tax, subtracting debits from credits, which means that in theory such processing could be done just as well on the workstation as on the server.

There is a school of thought that client/server design is best approached by assuming that the application code will run on the workstation, and that data will be stored centrally. Design proceeds by compromising on this position for the sort of reasons outlined above, and a whole set of considerations which fall under the heading of systems management.

2 Systems management

Systems management has at least as much to do with the shaping of a system as does its function, although there is a tendency to overlook it. Setting up an appropriate management environment is crucial to the successful running of any computer installation, from the very smallest to the very largest. Disaster-recovery procedures are obviously important to a bank, but so they are to the window cleaner who keeps a client list on a portable PC: if the laptop drops into the window cleaner's bucket of water, he has a disaster on his hands, which could conceivably drive him out of business.

Systems management issues will also increase the real cost of a system. There is sometimes a resistance to including such costs, but it is dangerous to ignore them.

Systems management is well understood in the world of central systems – most of the large operational computer systems today are based on IBM mainframe technology, and they have to deliver high levels of availability day in and day out. Mainframes are in some ways easier to manage than client/server systems: for example, there is no software distribution to worry about, because the terminals need no software. They do suffer from a high level of software complexity at the centre, though, which they handle by insisting on rigorous testing of every change that is made to the system. It is this very testing that accounts in part for the apparent inflexibility of such systems.

Systems management comprises

- User support
- Problem management
- Change management
- Availability management
- Security management
- Asset management
- Software distribution
- Disaster-recovery planning
- Capacity planning and performance management

These topics are, of course, interrelated: poor performance could be reported as a problem, could be the result of a change, and may cause capacity estimates to be revised. However, each is worth tackling separately for every size of system. The disaster-recovery plan for the window-cleaner's PC will be much simpler than for the bank's data centre, but they should both exist. It is also necessary to review these aspects with each new system that is installed, for it may impose new strains on the existing management infrastructure which require it to be upgraded.

User support

Assistance for users should be provided in a number of ways:

1. *Good interface design*. Attention paid to making the system genuinely easy to use is worth the investment. Powerful workstations provide an environment which can deliver excellent interfaces, which are an important feature of client/server systems. This is a new skill, and positively is *not* synonymous with dazzling colours and endless pop-up panels. It is to do with consistency, both within the system and with the rest of the user's environment. It is to do with encouragement for the user to explore new facilities, secure in the knowledge that he or she will be warned before any irrevocable actions are taken. It is to do with the provision of adequate help facilities.

2. *Adequate training*. This can be expensive, especially if users have to be taken away from their jobs for any period of time. As a result, it is often skimped, which endangers the success of the system. Training can often be provided via the workstation, particularly with the approach of multimedia capability.

    Much is spoken of intuitive interfaces, as one of the benefits of the graphical possibilities of the workstation. However, to the average person a VGA screen covered in icons together with a mouse and its pointer do not provide the basis of an intuitive interface. What *is* true is that once a person has grasped the basics of GUIs, and knows what to expect from the action bar, and from icons, that person is well equipped to absorb a new application function as it is added. That means that the first introduction to GUIs should be planned and thorough.

3. *Help facilities built into the system*. One of the rules about good user interfaces is that they should provide support at every level: from an overall description of the general purpose of the system to the alternatives for completing a particular field on the screen. A powerful workstation provides an excellent environment within which to provide extensive help. But is expensive and is again liable to be skimped – especially when deadlines approach.

4. *Reference documentation.* There is still a place for reference manuals and cards even with extensive help facilities.
5. *Helpdesk support.* In a system of any size it is likely that a central helpdesk is a worthwhile investment. Again, it is an expense. Interestingly, central helpdesks can find life more difficult with powerful workstations than with dumb terminals, because a user has so much more freedom to navigate around the system, and to use several facilities at once. Describing what's on the screen can be difficult for a user who has been opening windows on his or her workstation with reckless abandon. One answer to this is provided by mechanisms which allow the helpdesk to call up onto their own screen a replica of the user's screen, or indeed to take control from the user and sort it out.

    The helpdesk should be prepared to handle every sort of question from users – asking them to differentiate between communications problems and application problems, for example, does not work and leads to irritated users. It may well be that the helpdesk forwards the query to some specialist for a response, but the issue should always be handled through the same telephone number.

Problem management

In a system of any size there will be a number of problems outstanding at any point in time. Some of these will be genuine malfunctions, some will be misunderstandings or the result of a lack of training. It is important that *all* these should be cleared up, and not just left. A formal problem management process which logs all reported problems and tracks them until they are satisfactorily resolved has much to recommend it, not least the history file that is built up which can be analyzed for patterns, or used for reference when dealing with new problems.

There is no magic here – packages to record, track and report on problems are available, and can themselves be good examples of client/server technology at work. What needs to be behind them, however, is a simple management discipline, to set standards for the resolution of problems, to review problems regularly, to chase outstanding issues raised by persistent problems. Such management is well within the reach of a non-technical manager.

Change management

Change is the enemy of availability. The first question any engineer will ask when diagnosing faults is 'What has changed recently?' The centralized system is particularly prone to problems caused by change for two reasons, both related to the fact that everything runs on the same processor:

- There is a high level of change
- Every component of the system – both hardware and software – must interface properly with every other component for the system to function. This means that packages must all be at the right release levels, and the hardware at the right change levels.

Client/server systems change this situation by breaking systems down into specialist components and distributing function around the system, thereby reducing the change level at each component. However, the components still have to work together. So this is not to say that change management is no longer required, merely that it is arguably less crucial. In some ways, change management is more difficult. For example, changing the software in 250 workstations is a significant task which needs suitable software distribution tools and considerable planning.

One of the important benefits of client/server design is that function tends to be provided in the form of flexible tools, rather than of pre-scribed, pre-coded functions. This puts more flexibility into the hands of the users, and allows them to deal with many change requirements without any software or hardware change. For example, changing the layout of a report should not require intervention from central programming resources, it should be handled by the user, and is unlikely to cause any changes to hardware or software.

It remains true that every planned change to the system should be examined for its likely impact on availability, that multiple simultaneous changes should be avoided, and that mechanisms to 'back out' changes should be at the ready. This last point is important even in the smallest system. It is quite possible to render a single PC system totally useless by wrongly installing a new operating system, for example, and then finding oneself with no way of recovering, short of a humiliating call to the local dealer.

Change in most computer systems is to be expected as an ongoing phenomenon: in centralized systems that change is occasionally traumatic and involves shutting down the entire operation. In distributed systems this is less likely – an important benefit.

Availability management

Target availability levels should be one of the fundamental design aims of a system. Total availability is as elusive as total security – but must still be the ultimate goal. Most hardware platforms that are sold for very high availability are based on standby components which take over when the primary fails. While this approach does indeed deliver very high avail-ability, there is still the chance that while the primary component is broken, the backup will fail. It is also clear that providing backup components and the mechanism to detect errors and to switch over will more than double the cost of the system. Justifying this additional cost to raise availability from say 95% to 97% is not always easy: especially given the fact that the quality of hardware available today is very high.

Manufacturers are achieving this first, by sheer attention to quality processes – we have much to thank the Japanese for here. Second, they are building in recovery capability, even at the chip level. Third, they are including diagnostic capability that allows repair action to be very swift.

Overall availability of a system must be measured at the user's end of the system – this is the only availability that ultimately matters. That figure is the result of a string of individual component availabilities, which must also be measured, to spot problems with a particular product or supplier.

Client/server systems differ from centralized systems in some interesting ways. First, there is less chance of a total system blackout, because the workstation itself is powerful enough to provide some residual facilities. A customer order can still be accepted, subject to later verification, even if the stock system and the order processing system have died, provided the workstation is suitably equipped.

Second, the more function is distributed over a number of servers, the more protected the user is from total failure, so here again is a decision for the designer: what is the optimum degree of distribution?

Third, the workstation itself is probably the most critical component for the user – if it fails, the user is helpless, and the workstation is probably the least reliable component in the system, if only because it is exposed to abuse of various sorts. Consequently, the designer must have a plan for dealing quickly with failed workstations – most likely by having standby machines. In turn, this means avoiding using the workstation as the location for permanent, important business data.

Lastly, they can exploit the phenomenon that the most reliable computer systems are those which are handling a particular task for which they are well designed, and which are not subjected to high rates of change. A server whose job is to handle electronic mail, for example, and which does no more than this is likely to be more reliable than a central system which is handling not only mail but also printing, database searches and so forth. Set against this, of course, is the fact that to provide a complete set of facilities to a user, one will need many servers up and running simultaneously. However, overall, a system designed from specialized components is likely to be more robust than one general-purpose computer.

High availability means not only a long MTBF but also a short MTTR. Lowering the time to repair is achieved in two basic ways: either negotiating hard with the organization that is handling the servicing of the system, and listening to their recommendations about equipment, or providing standby capability, which costs money.

As we have already said, standby equipment is probably appropriate for workstations, because they are relatively cheap and numerous, so that one standby machine per location may be adequate. Standby equipment is also the usual mechanism within telecommunication facilities – often provided by the telecommunications company – but it may not be cost-effective when talking about a large database server. In that case, the quality of the equipment selected is crucial, as is the availability of spares and the capability of the engineers. Modern database servers provide facilities such as disk mirroring or RAID technology which significantly improve availability without necessarily doubling the cost.

Security management

Security is about allowing ready access to facilities to those who are entitled to them, and preventing access to those who are not. Total security is probably not achievable, although it remains a goal. High levels of security also tend to impose a high level of overhead on users and systems alike, which may be more than a commercial organization is willing to bear. Once again, the designer must select a level of security which is adequate, practical and affordable.

Security in client/server systems raises some new problems: the essence of a client/server architecture is that services may be provided on a variety of servers, rather than one central system. This could mean that users need to identify themselves to each server individually, clearly impractical for more than two or three services, especially if they each require a separate password.

The current thinking on addressing this problem revolves around the concept of another special server which handles security matters for the whole system. Users must log onto this server first, which provides them with a key to the other servers to which they have rights of access. International standards around this solution are emerging as are products which implement it. Clearly, standards are required in this area if servers from a variety of sources are to be welded into a coherent system.

Depending on the level of security required, and the complexity of the system, local solutions to the security problem can be designed and built. Access to particularly sensitive information, for example, could be managed by holding it on a totally separate server to which only the right people are physically connected (this was the solution adopted by a large corporation to protect its directors' emoluments from the eyes of the populace).

In all the excitement over high-tech security mechanisms, however, it should be remembered that, as with household security, relatively simple measures will keep out all but determined intruders. In many cases of external penetration of computer systems, it has been achieved by acquiring a modem telephone number, using well-known access ids delivered with the software for installation purposes and never removed, and trying old favourite passwords, such as 'password'.

Basic management attention to the basics will increase security enormously. Remove unused access identifiers, ensure passwords are kept secret and changed regularly, limit public dial-in access to the minimum.

It is a sad fact that much illegal activity is carried out by authorized users: dishonest or disgruntled employees. This can best be spotted by monitoring activity within the system and identifying changes or unusual behaviour. It is a subject in its own right, and not particularly a problem for client/server systems.

Database servers provide a useful additional layer of security through facilities for restricting access to data based on the user id. Such facilities are already well understood in the centralized systems world.

Physical security is important, too. A benefit of workstations is that they are increasingly portable – which means they are easy to steal. They should not, therefore, be used to store passwords or other access information.

Software distribution

This is an area where centralized systems score heavily over distributed systems. The distribution of software to hundreds of workstations is a major undertaking, which is simply not needed on mainframe systems with their simple, software-free terminals. There is an increasing number of packages available on the market to handle this task, which will need to be evaluated. Ideally, such a package will provide facilities to 'push' software down to the workstations from a central point, as well as allowing workstations to 'pull' it down on demand. It will provide for remote installation and rollback, as well as central accounting functions to keep track of which workstations have which releases of what software.

Asset management

A client/server system is typically built from components that have a commercial value in themselves, such as servers, workstations and software. These components are likely to be scattered throughout an organization and beyond, into employees' homes and cars. Asset management is the process by which these assets are recorded and maintained and is therefore an important activity for client/server systems.

It is important to know what assets the company has tied up in its computer systems not only for accounting purposes but also for ensuring that they are all at the right level of software, that they have on them the software they need, and no more, that they are properly cared for and protected by insurance. Detailed information about configurations is also important for problem diagnosis.

Again, there is little magic associated with this requirement – it is a matter of basic management attention, assisted by an appropriate computer system. There are software packages available to assist with asset management, some of which are usefully linked to software distribution systems, for example. Such a system can help ensure that a company is paying for the correct number of software licences at the most favourable tariff. It is clearly an area where client/server systems have a greater need of focus than centralized terminal-based systems, because the value of assets outside the computer room is likely to be much higher.

Disaster-recovery planning

As with making a will, this is something we tend to avoid, although we know we should do it. Every computer system of every complexion should have a disaster-recovery plan associated with it, which is to say, a plan of action in the event that an unforeseen event destroys a significant part of the system. It is particularly important in circumstances where the computer system represents a single point of failure for the whole organization. Many companies today would be extremely embarrassed if they lost their computer system and some would collapse entirely.

This is not always true: an analysis of an insurance company showed that in the event of a total failure of the computer systems no claims could be settled, no bills could be paid, but premium income would continue to arrive via the banking system. In other words, they would actually be better off financially! Eventually, their customers would complain about the lack of service, and no new policies could be sold, but it was clear that they could survive for a significant period – perhaps a month – before there was any major impact on the business.

By contrast, if an airline lost its reservations and, more important, its 'departure control' system, the impact would be immediate.

Highly centralized systems are more exposed to disasters than distributed systems, for the obvious reason that a single explosion or power outage is unlikely to shut down all the systems if they are dispersed. One of the design decisions for a client/server system is how distributed a system it should be: and one of the factors to take into account is how important is survival through a disaster.

A disaster-recovery plan is not necessarily very complex: we mentioned a window cleaner and his portable PC earlier in the book. His disaster-recovery plan would be very simple: acquire another PC, reinstall the software, load the data from the backup and carry on. (Notice, by the way, that this makes dropping his PC less of a disaster than losing the paper notebook that it no doubt replaced.)

It may be even be a conscious decision to make no special arrangements. If the business runs within a single building, for example, then a disaster which destroys the computer will also probably destroy the building, shutting down the entire business. What is important is to have thought through the impact of a disaster occurring to the computer system and then to devise suitable plans for handling the situation. If this combination is unacceptable, a redesign of the system is called for.

Perhaps the database can be split between servers, or replicated across them. Perhaps services can be split across several servers, in different locations, rather then concentrated on one. But perhaps splitting services does not, in fact, reduce the impact significantly. Is losing half of the customer database any better than losing all of it?

An important parameter is one of time: in the event of any disaster, how long do you have to recover before the business fails? The second important parameter is: which parts of my system are truly vital? Usually, customer records fall under the heading of 'vital', whereas stock information may not. This allows the designer to focus attention on designing a system and a plan to allow the vital parts of the system to be recovered within the survival period.

Capacity planning and performance management

Both capacity planning and performance management are important and difficult tasks in the centralized computer world. Important because upgrading a central system is usually an expensive undertaking, and therefore to be deferred as long as possible. Difficult because all aspects of the system are running on a single central computer, which means that not only must the individual components be measured for growth but also the interactions between those elements must be allowed for. If, for example, the number of users of a centralized system is increased, not only will the terminal handling software demand more memory and more processor cycles but so will the application software and the database software. The combined shortage of memory may increase paging levels, which in turn burns processor cycles.

In theory, at least, upgrading a client/server system should be more manageable, more predictable and less expensive. Let us examine the case of the increased number of users to see why.

When new users are added to the system either they are given a new workstation or their old ones are upgraded to handle the new tasks. Ideally, this upgrade will simply involve the granting of additional permissions to allow users access to new facilities. However, it may involve physically installing new software on the existing workstation, which may in turn involve upgrading the workstation's memory or processor speed. *Whatever is involved, it is handled quite independently of the network and the servers.*

At the server end there will clearly be a higher level of demand, but because the server is only handling its particular range of services – e.g.

SQL access to a database – the impact of the increased load is more easily predicted. If the server is running in a multiprocessor or, better yet, a parallel environment, an upgrade closely tailored to the requirement can be added. (This granularity of client/server systems is one of their attractions.) Again, any such upgrade is handled independently of the network and the workstation. In both cases the communication links must be checked to ensure that they are capable of handling the increased load. We shall address the issues of telecommunications in a separate chapter.

The move to client/server is not happening in a vacuum – indeed it is driven partly by the falling cost of computer hardware. In parallel, the cost of telecommunications is falling, while the capability is increasing dramatically – we will discuss this more in a later chapter. One often-cited reason for moving towards client/server systems is precisely to exploit this explosive growth in capability. The result is that the cost of hardware and telecommunication links is declining significantly as a fraction of the overall system cost. The costs and capabilities are expected to continue along their respective growth curves for the foreseeable future, which will take us to the point where it no longer makes sense to haggle over whether a workstation should be Pentium-based or not, or whether the LAN should be 16Mb or 100Mb per second.

Architects today do not attempt to save money by reducing the bandwidth of the sewage system in a building – the saving in cost is not worth the potential problems. Soon it will be the same with LANs. A LAN will be installed that is adequate to meet comfortably the needs of the population who will use it. This is already almost true of workstations – a 6MB 486-based system will comfortably handle the personal needs of most commercial users today.

In fact, if the movement of formatted data (by which I mean EBCDIC or ASCII characters) is adequate to meet the needs of a business, one could already specify workstations and telecommunication links which would, with a high degree of certainty, meet the needs of the users indefinitely. As with sewage, there is a limited demand that one user can place on the system.

What the restriction excludes, of course, is image, graphical and voice data, all of which imply heavy loads on the transport mechanism. We shall have to wait some years to see how useful such technologies really are, and for the arrival of workstations and LANs which will handle it comfortably.

In short, the business of capacity planning for workstations and networks will – over time – decline to that of installing the necessary bandwidth at the time an office block is built, with the intent that no further attention will be needed, other than routine maintenance and the handling of the occasional blockage.

Capacity planning for servers will be handled much as electricity is supplied today. The providers monitor usage, charge their users based on their individual usage, identify patterns and trends, and plan upgrades to meet predicted demands. It is not a requirement of the electricity company that every sale of an electrical appliance is notified to them, and the same will be true of computer service suppliers: they too will have to rely on patterns and trends.

This usage monitoring will need to extend beyond simply watching the needle flicker on the database-utilization gauge. It is also important to monitor what requests are being made, by trapping SQL, for example – and optimizing the use of indexes, and other tuning mechanisms. Poor use of the language can also be spotted in this way.

The analogy with electricity suppliers provides another essential item for server management – overload protection. It is vital that sudden, unexpected demands on the system are avoided, and handled sensibly if they occur. This is achieved in the electricity industry by the use of fuses and cut-outs, which cut off the supply to any user who makes excessive demands. Precisely the same sort of control will almost certainly be needed by servers, since they will be prey to accidental or even deliberate demands of an excessive size.

An obvious example of this is provided again by the database server, which could be overwhelmed by a syntactically correct SQL request to join every row of a multi-million-row table to every other row in the same table. Such enormous demands must be intercepted and handled by the server.

On the other side of the coin, performance management will need to be done as a housekeeping item for networks, to ensure that they are running smoothly and to diagnose any problems that occur. It will be an important part of the planning for server growth – the performance of the server will be an important indicator of its status and of its need for attention.

Some performance problems are perceptual rather than actual – that is, a user may feel that the system is being unresponsive because his or her expectations are incorrect. This situation can be addressed in several ways: educate the users in the demands that they are placing on the system, ensure that the system informs the user when significant workloads are being undertaken, and check the helpdesk staff ask the right questions when dealing with a disgruntled user. A mixture of all these techniques is recommended.

The disciplines of systems management are well understood in the mainframe environment, which has been supporting 'mission-critical' systems for a long time. The need for systems management is just as important for client/server systems: in some regards, it is more arduous, due to the distributed nature of the system. Being arduous, it is also an expense, but failure to plan properly for the management of client/server systems will lead ultimately to disappointment.

3 System design

Design overview

In discussing design of client/server systems we are principally concerned with those systems where the client and server processes reside on different platforms, linked by a communications system, with functionality and data distributed between them, rather than the more general case (where components of any type interact as client and/or server). In the general case of client/server architecture, the user requirements and logical architecture of a system can be modelled at any level using components which interact as client and server. Allied with object-oriented architectures, this produces a powerful technique for logical design.

A system can be described in terms of components, or objects, each of which may provide a service (or services) or make use of services, or both. The components can reflect the business or user functions, segmented by functional area or procedures, and can be chosen to allow flexibility and future scalability.

Each component carries out well-defined functionality and this functionality may involve both data and algorithms. A component can provide a service to others, and make use of services offered by other components.

A component communicates with others through well-defined interfaces. Ideally, these interfaces will conform to published standards to allow interworking with components from other suppliers. Interfaces may be via message passing, or procedure calls, and should be unconcerned with physical locations of components.

How a component implements its functionality is unimportant; the method is encapsulated within the component. This allows changes or improvements to be made without affecting the other components which interface with it.

With the use of transparent 'middleware' to provide communications between components the mapping from a logical design based on client and server components to a physical design should be relatively straight-forward. Middleware can vary in its level of sophistication, for example simply passing through database accesses, or converting between different DBMS interfaces, or providing full on-line transaction processing (OLTP) facilities (see Appendix 2 for a discussion of transaction processing).

Ideally, when designing a system the physical layout should only become important when carrying out physical design. The logical design and the preceding analysis should be unchanged, and therefore existing methodologies can potentially be used for client/server platform solutions. In practice, the target architecture (or significant parts of it) can be given either as a constraint on the solution or as part of the problem. Even then it should not have a significant impact on logical design, but will be considered during logical design to make translation to physical design more effective. Physical design can possibly be treated as a mapping of logical objects (e.g. parts of presentation, application, database) to physical locations (e.g. on client or server platforms).

Architecture and infrastructure design

An important stage in design is to determine the system architecture and define the underlying infrastructure. In practice, the architecture is the arrangement of client platform, server platform and network and the outline split of functionality and data (presentation, application and database components) between client and server platforms. The infrastructure is the hardware and system software (e.g. runtime support, operating system, database, network) required to support that architecture.

There a number of different ways in which the architecture of a client/server system can be defined. The differences between the varieties is in how the presentation, application and database components of the system are distributed between the client and server platforms.

The presentation component (P) is that part of the system concerned with interfacing to the outside world, whether to a human user or other computer system. The presentation could take the form of screen or printed output, data transfer (e.g. file transfer, fax or modem).

The application component (A) is concerned with the user-defined functionality from whatever viewpoint the user takes. For a manager this might be spreadsheet calculations or the company accounting system. For a printer manufacturer it might be the page description language interpreter. The database component (D) contains the user data and the database management system. Components reside on platforms ([ ]) which comprise the hardware and system software required to support them.

The symbols in parentheses are from the LEGHAWK notation which can be used to describe client/server architectures and systems. Examples of LEGHAWK will be used throughout this chapter to concisely describe the various architectures discussed. A full description of LEGHAWK is given in Appendix 2.

Figure 3.1 shows the main possibilities for arranging these components on client and server platforms. We have ignored the two extreme cases where all components are situated on the same platform (as neither platform is then either a client or a server). Taking each other case in turn:

1. *Distributed presentation [P]~[PAD].* In such architectures the presentation component is split between client platform and server platform, with application and database components located entirely on the server platform. An example of such a system is where an improved (GUI) presentation is added to an existing legacy system, and communicates via a terminal emulation (e.g. 3270) to the original character mode presentation component of the legacy system. This approach maximizes the existing investment in a system while improving usability.

2. *Separate presentation [P]~[AD].* Here the presentation component is located entirely on the client platform, with application and database entirely on the server. This approach allows good use to be made of relatively low-cost workstations which support GUI presentation software. X-Windows presentation, driven from a remote application, is a common example.

3. *Separate database [PA]~[D].* Here both presentation and application are located entirely on the client platform with only the database held on the server. This is probably the most common client/server architecture currently in use as it is supported by many vendors of DBMS and user tools. An example might be an Executive Information System (EIS) where data from a corporate database can be accessed using off-the-shelf analysis tools or custom applications. This approach makes existing or new databases available to end-users through easy-to-use tools at relatively low software cost.

4. *Distributed application [PA]~[AD].* In this case, presentation and part of the application are located on the client, with the database and the rest of the application located on the server. The application functionality may be split vertically (i.e. each function is entirely on one of client or server) or horizontally (where some part of the function is on the client and communicates with the other part on the server). Typically, the split will be a combination of the two, with at least a trigger being communicated from client application to server application. This approach allows functions to be located on the most appropriate platform and an interface to be defined at an appropriate (business transaction) level, perhaps hiding server implementation details from the client.

5. *Distributed database [PAD]~[D].* This places both presentation and application entirely on the client platform, with the database split between platforms. Data can be split vertically (i.e. different tables on each platform) or horizontally (different rows from tables on different

Figure 3.1
Categories of client/
server architecture.

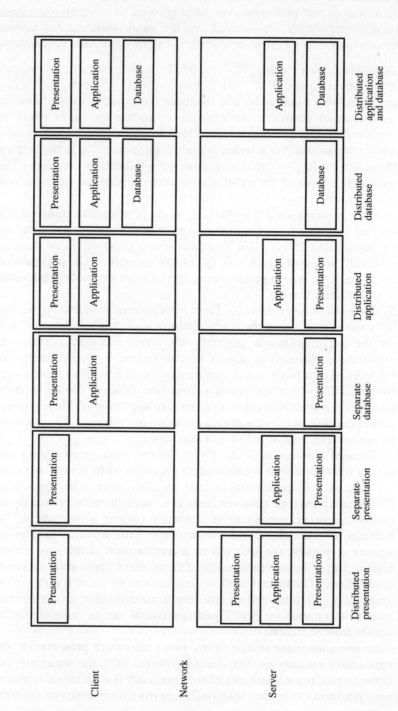

platforms), or replicated (some data appearing on both platforms). There may well be a combination of all three. This approach allows data to be placed where most appropriate, particularly to improve performance by placing data near to where it will be used, at a cost of more involved data management.

6. *Distributed application and database [PAD]~[AD]*. Here, both application and database are split across platforms, with the presentation entirely on the client. This can be seen as a combination of the distributed application and distributed database architectures and is a more general case. Ideally, the components can be moved from one platform to another transparently. It is the ultimate client/server architecture with maximum flexibility to change.

There are other possible combinations with two platforms, plus architectures involving more than two platforms. However, such architectures are either unlikely in practice (e.g. [PD]~[A]) or can be treated as combinations of the above (e.g. [P]~[A]~[D] appears as [P]~[AD] from the viewpoint of the [P] platform, or [PA]~[D] from the [D] platform, or both from the point of view of the [A] platform). Of the six main architectures, practical examples can be split into two major types.

Executive Information Systems [PA]~[D] (Type 3)

EIS require analysis and presentation of raw data that has been consolidated in some way. Often data is modelled and what-if scenarios played against these models. The analysis requirements are highly changeable as new management techniques and monitoring methods evolve and move in and out of fashion. From an architectural requirements point of view:

- Speed of data access is not critical. A few minutes to download a set of data to manipulate for analysis and modelling is not unacceptable. *Ad hoc* enquiries should be faster, but need not be within the 1–3 second response times required for OLTP systems.
- EIS systems do not generally update the data. The use of raw SQL without integrity and validity checks is therefore acceptable, though stored procedures and business rules could enrich the services provided by the database.
- The SQL queries are often not known in advance, so the client process must be capable of building Dynamic SQL. By working in conjunction with the users, the DBA can help access speeds by maintaining heavily indexed views of the data.
- The client processes are on the workstation or PC, so that they can take advantage of the sophisticated formatting and presentation techniques available. In EIS, the presentation and formatting of the data is tightly

linked to the application itself, and should reside on the same processor. EIS client processes will have their own presentation methods built in, or take advantage of third-party products. There are a lot of commercially available EIS products for workstations that only require SQL access to data. Some form of high-level programming (such as macros) tailors the interface to build the client applications.

On-line Transaction Processing [P]~[AD] (Type 2) and [PA]~[AD] (Type 4)

OLTP systems have the following characteristics:

- Many users using the same application
- Transactions are usually short
- Data accesses are predictable
- Fast user response time is essential (sometimes the user has a customer on the phone)
- Data integrity is very important

OLTP systems are usually implemented by application servers running on the same platform as the database. As the servers are waiting for client requests, there is no overhead in program loading, initialization and the SQL parsing required for some database interfaces. The servers are responsible for data integrity and can perform complex validation against business rules before committing data to the database. The transaction commit cycle ensures that the database is consistent as all, or none, of the transaction is performed. Indexing for easy access of the data must be matched against the need to update these indices when data is added the system or changed. As the SQL performed is predictable, careful database tuning becomes possible.

Most client server systems require concepts from both the EIS and OLTP models. Off-the-shelf client server systems tend to concentrate on the EIS requirement, as it is comparatively simple to implement, and there is a clear demand for it from the business community. OLTP systems are much harder to implement, but once the application servers are in place, they can offer a higher level of abstraction to EIS enquiry client tasks, as they can supply information about business objects, rather than simply database tables.

For example, a careful analysis of a requirement might skew the split between EIS and OLTP in unexpected ways. A system for a group of retail stores may be happy to have all the data from stores downloaded at the end of each day, and new indices built on the data overnight for complex enquiries on the next day. It could be mainly an EIS system, with little need for immediate updates.

Examples of client platforms

In practice client platforms typically fall into one of the following categories.

Terminal client [P]

A terminal client contains solely a presentation component, for example an X-Windows workstation, block-mode terminal or 'glass teletype'. It could be a display-only device (e.g. a scoreboard or airport departures video screen) or an input-only device (e.g. a security pass reader or temperature sensor).

Personal platform client [PA] or [P]

A personal platform is a PC or workstation with (typically) a GUI, and possibly application(s) used by a single (human) user. It will contain a presentation component, and usually an application component.

Machine controller [PA]

This type of client will contain some form of external interfacing (e.g. sensors and actuators) plus some application functionality to control or monitor the interface, for example an outstation of a control system. It will contain a presentation component (the interface) and an application component.

Examples of server platforms

In practice, server platforms typically fall into one of the following categories.

File server [D]

A file server can be used to centralize documents, drawings or multimedia presentations. Groupware or workflow software can be the client process that controls access to the data. Even simple file locking and sharing mechanisms may provide enough control in some cases. The server contains a database component (i.e. the file system) and may include some application components (e.g. Groupware as a NLM on a Novell server).

Database server [D]

A database server typically provides data by responding to SQL requests. This implies that the client process must understand the structure of the data and the way it is held on the database. Each SQL statement is an interaction between client and server. The server contains a database component (i.e. the DBMS).

Enhanced database server [AD]

Some database servers will also provide the ability to package up a set of SQL statements that accepts parameters. This provides an extra layer of abstraction to the client processes, as the underlying SQL need not be known. Also, integrity rules can be built into some database servers – e.g. delete on a customer record will fail if it has outstanding transactions. The server contains both a database component (DBMS) and application component (procedures and rules).

Application servers [AD] or [A]

A single client request is translated into complex business logic, and a series of database accesses may take place. The commit cycle will ensure the integrity of the database within a single transaction on a DBMS. Application servers can access data from remote sources, initiate downloads, produce reports, etc. They are not restricted to a single database. The server contains an application component, and possibly a database component.

Presentation server [P] or [AP]

A printer is an example of a presentation server; it presents output in response to a client request. Other presentation servers could be faxes, scanners or modems. These servers may have embedded intelligence which from some points of view would be an application component.

Architectural issues

Although client/server is a recently emerged approach to system architecture it does not in itself have many new issues to be considered. What it does do is bring together several particular approaches each of which have their own issues. These include:

- Distributed systems of computers linked by LANs or WANs
- Distributed databases
- Distributed functionality

- Open systems
- Graphical, windowed interfaces and multimedia
- Relational DBMS
- Down-sizing or right-sizing
- Working together of software and/or hardware from different vendors

For example:

- Any use of distributed data or processing across nodes in a network, and the consequences with respect to data integrity and data security. This is not specifically a client/server problem, but one with distributed systems in general. Ideally, it should be possible to rely on the DBMS Application server to ensure data integrity and security, with the use of two-phase commit for distributed updates, if these are necessary.
- At the functional level, the location of a client and a server on the same or different nodes in a network should not be important as communication between them can be handled by communications software which can hide the locations. However, in practice, communication between client and server on the same node is usually faster and more reliable than communication between different nodes. In both cases, however, communication errors must be handled. Communication between nodes can be made more reliable at the cost of speed, with available bandwidth reduced by error-correction codes or retransmission of corrupted messages. Slow speed of communications can affect design, as some designs may produce unacceptably reduced performance over slow communications links. Again, this is not specifically a client/server problem, but client/server systems tend to be networked.

Choosing an architecture

The choice of architecture may be limited in many ways, some technical, others not, and may be flavoured by existing hardware, software and communications. It may be impossible to justify the expense of replacing existing hardware even if it would give a better result. Many users already have PCs (IBM-compatible or Mac), and an office LAN is now much more common. There may well be existing mini or mainframe systems which can act as servers, if they have sufficient capacity to support the new application and its users (perhaps by removing an application that is to be replaced). The possibility of upgrading existing equipment has also to be considered, rather than replacing equipment which cannot provide the appropriate capacity. If equipment is reaching the end of its useful life, or is becoming expensive to maintain, it may be worth taking the opportunity to replace it.

The design may also be limited by the existing infrastructure. It may be necessary to use an existing DBMS, as well as the operating system of existing hardware. An existing network may limit the protocols used (perhaps as a result of use of routers acting at transport levels), and possibly the traffic volumes. The speed of the network could be a major factor in determining the split of data and functionality between client and server.

If there is a choice of new hardware and software, there may well still be limitations imposed by corporate strategies, existing skill base, requirements to interconnect, etc. There may be a policy of selecting only 'open' systems or systems from existing suppliers.

Example: A small system to centralize data for some PCs

Where a small number of staff work together but have their own data on their own PCs there may be some benefit in centralizing this data into a shared database. The PCs could be connected by a LAN to a server containing the database. Database access tools would be provided for each user's PC.

The tools for small client server systems are best bought off the shelf. If there are not many users updating the system, then there isn't the need to invest in OLTP mechanisms. A package like Microsoft's Access across a LAN to the database on the server is an example. Programming of the front-end tools would be necessary.

Example: An on-line enquiry system

There is a need for staff at branch offices to have access to the current data from a corporate database. They already have PCs with a local LAN for file and printer services in each branch. The database is on the corporate mainframe at head office.

Our architecture could use existing PCs and LANs, linking the LANs back to the mainframe at head office over a WAN. Presentation and some application functionality on the PCs would trigger stored query procedures in the mainframe database. The results would be sent back to the PC for display. Since users need the latest data from the database, data cannot be cached at the branch offices, so all queries access the database directly.

Our infrastructure requires hardware and several layers of communications software to link the LANs to the mainframe allowing the queries to be sent and results transferred back. The DBMS on the server requires the ability to store procedures, and allow access from remote sites, with a reasonable performance. The PCs will require application software to trigger the appropriate queries and display the results in the appropriate format.

Architecture design considerations

Level of client/server interaction

A vital design decision is the level at which client and server platforms will interact, effectively placing the system into an architectural category described earlier. The choice will be narrowed by the interfaces offered by system software such as the DBMS and the protocols supported by the platforms and network.

If migrating from an existing system, the interface may be dictated by the requirements to minimize, or avoid completely, changes to the existing applications. For example, an existing mainframe application may call for a terminal emulation interface or communication via file transfer to an existing database. This would be a Type 1 [P]~[PAD] distributed presentation architecture. See Chapter 5 for more information on migration.

A DBMS may provide its own proprietary remote access protocol (e.g. Oracle's SQL*Net), usually supporting interaction at SQL or DBMS transaction level (Type 3 [PA]~[D]), perhaps by triggering stored procedures (Type 4 [PA]~[AD]). Alternatively, third-party middleware may be available to provide the appropriate communication.

It may be appropriate to construct an application-specific interface on top of a network protocol. This interface could be at the level of application transactions (e.g. data query) or application functions (e.g. trigger end of day). If building a system from scratch, with no existing systems to dictate an approach, then these same choices are available, but can be applied more flexibly.

It is good practice (in any architecture design) to layer the system – for example, to simplify application software functions by hiding the intricacies of network interfacing in a library or a third-party package. In client/server architectures the correct layering is crucial to the success of the system. The foundation of a client/server system is the infrastructure software (the network software, DBMS and middleware) which handles the complexities of a distributed environment and hides it from the application software. If the foundation is designed correctly and its interfaces well defined, then changes to the environment should not mean changes to the application software.

There may well be more than one (type of) client and server in the system. For example, special-purpose server applications may be used to provide certain functionality (e.g. graphics display, statistical analysis) on client or server platform. Data exchange with other applications (e.g. Cut & Paste, DDE) will require interfaces with other clients or servers. If these are bought in, the interfaces will be determined by the vendor. If developed specially, the level of interaction has to be considered carefully.

Whichever level of interface is chosen, it will usually manifest itself to the code being developed as an application programming interface (API), although some interfaces may make use of embedded code with a pre-processor to generate API calls (e.g. embedded SQL). Ideally, the interface will provide transparency of location, so that application code need not concern itself with an underlying network and possibly transparency of the DBMS in use to improve portability.

Platform

The platform is an overall term for the hardware and system software on which the system is to be implemented. It is possible to treat the hardware and software as one item as applications are more concerned with the support offered by the system software than with the actual machine architecture, provided the right physical devices (disks, network interface) are available.

The choice of platform for client and server may not be a choice at all. The existing client platforms may have to be used, particularly if there are already a large number of users equipped with them. For the server, it may be required to make use of an existing system (mainframe or mini) or it may be possible to obtain a new one. The policies of an IT department are likely to be more applicable to the choice of server, as is the availability of existing skilled staff to support and operate the server. There may be policies on choice of hardware vendor, operating system and system software, DBMS and communications and a required level of 'openness' or interoperability. The policies will have been determined on the basis of experience, existing systems, or future strategy, taking into account such considerations as the IT marketplace, vendor support and stability, price/performance ratios and scalability (up and down), product availability (including multiple sources), support for other system software (e.g. DBMS), networking support, interoperability and adherence to standards. These policies may not, however, be appropriate to a new client/server system if it is the first to be implemented in the organization, so some negotiation may be required to modify or obtain a 'step-out' from the standard policies.

It is likely that the chosen platforms will have to support various standards currently deemed to be 'open', such as a UNIX- or POSIX-based operating system for servers, GUI windows-like interface for clients, TCP/IP (or perhaps OSI) communications, ANSI standard languages, SQL (relational) DBMS. Appropriate access control and data security features will be required too.

Whether using existing platforms or new ones, the performance of those platforms must be considered. Will they have enough power to support the anticipated volumes of users, data and transactions, allowing for some growth? Will they support all the applications to be implemented on them, including known future ones? Some capacity planning will have to be carried out, with possibly some benchmark testing, in order to determine the required CPU, memory, I/O and disk capacities required. The chosen platform should also have the ability to support upgrades as more capacity is required, or to be scalable up to larger systems without changing the application.

Network

Connectivity has already been discussed in general terms. Here are some other specific considerations.

If a network is already in place, it is likely that it will have to be used, provided that is practical. If a new network is to be installed then decisions will be required concerning the physical level (cabling and electrical interface), the transport protocol(s) to be used, and the higher-level protocols required to support the application. The systems to be connected, and the network they support will influence the choices. The type of usage of the systems (e.g. network file services, host terminal access), and the performance required (considering any existing and new loading) will determine factors like speed and topology. It may be appropriate to split a network into segments to limit impact of heavy traffic.

Another factor is the ability of buildings to accept the cabling required. A consideration of cabling is its ability to support future developments in network speed, types of data (images and sound as well as data), and new protocols. There is choice between copper cables (coax or twisted pair) or fiber optics.

Where local area networks in different sites have to be connected over a wide-area network, support for routers and bridges is an issue. Where LANs are separated by significant distances the use of wide-area private or public connections becomes necessary.

There are several standards at each level of the network, some corresponding to the ISO OSI 7 layer model, some proprietary, and some *de facto*. All other things being equal, it is best to go for standards at physical and transport levels. For example, Ethernet and TCP/IP are most popular with UNIX-based servers, and are widely available for client and server platforms. In an IBM environment, token ring and SNA may be more appropriate. It is often possible for several transport protocols to be used over a single physical network. It may be possible to hide the actual protocols in use from the application by selecting a high-level protocol which provides transparent support for several (e.g. Oracle's SQL*Net). Obtaining advice from a network specialist is highly recommended.

Presentation

The presentation is that part of the system which interfaces to the outside world. These days, when interfacing to a human, it is most likely to be a

GUI, except in certain specialist applications. The GUI will almost certainly use a Windows, Icons, Menus and Pointer (WIMP) metaphor.

When designing the presentation, the client platform may dictate an approach. If the client is to be a PC, then MS-Windows is an obvious candidate for a GUI; if it is a workstation then X-Windows; if a Macintosh then there is only one sensible choice. A GUI is almost compulsory at the moment, but it may not be appropriate (or practical) in some specialist circumstances. By using these standards you gain access to existing support software, device drivers etc. plus any new upgrades, and can use any compatible hardware without changing your application. You can also make use of built-in facilities for sharing data with or transferring data to other applications (e.g. OLE, DDE, Cut & Paste, import/export via standard file formats)

Use the corresponding *de facto* user interface standard, and follow the conventions associated with that standard, rather than invent your own. In this way, your application will work just like all the others on that platform, with the same look and feel. This reduces learning time, and frustration, for users familiar with other such applications. It can reduce the time taken by users to achieve the desired results (although it can give them the opportunity to waste time making output look pretty).

If there is to be more than one type of client platform you will need to consider how to cope with differences in look and feel. If you handle each one separately, will development and maintenance be too expensive? If a common approach is taken for all, will it mean using the lowest common denominator resulting in a poor implementation on all platforms, or a completely different look and feel? There are tools which can be used to implement a common approach which is mapped to different clients, but will they be good enough for you?

GUIs are built around a message-based architecture, with events sending messages which trigger actions. There is in-built support for multitasking. This architecture has implications for control of concurrency and database transactions. For example, one window could be displaying data being updated by another, or two windows could try to update the same data at the same time. A strategy has to be determined to resolve or prevent such conflicts (see below).

GUIs are particularly suited to prototyping, object-oriented techniques and rapid development methodologies and tools. It is relatively easy and quick to produce a working mock-up of a GUI presentation, using off-the-shelf tools. There are 4GLs and application generators, with ready-made presentation objects designed especially for this purpose, some supporting more than one target platform. Often they will include database front-ends to allow data to be easily obtained from the database.

Client/server systems can offer users an Object Oriented User Interface (OOUI). By presenting a model of the real world that has some correspondence with the user interface, users can more easily cope with the computerization of their daily tasks. Dragging a customer into an order may make intuitive sense. The customer object can have many 'views', and be packaged in with tasks, e.g. a customer object may be associated with an 'orders' task.

For OOUI to work well, the objects and tasks must map cleanly to a set of servers. That implies that some servers specialize in creation, amendment and viewing of business objects, and others with the application of these objects into tasks. With further analysis of a particular business application, it may be that the enquiry server APIs discussed below correspond to the object view as far as the client task is concerned.

Printing

Printing is a form of presentation which requires special consideration. Most systems produce printed output. In the traditional mainframe environment, line printers would be driven by the mainframe, possibly overnight and the output distributed each morning. In a client/server environment, printed output can be produced either by the client platform or by the server platform, and often by both. Users expect to be able to make *ad hoc* and immediate requests to produce reports or other printed output, and have it appear on their own laser printer, nicely formatted.

The main problem with the printing aspects of a system design is not that the requirements are difficult to meet but that they get forgotten. Driving a peripheral is not seen as a problem in a mainframe environment, and so system designers tend to ignore it.

Consider a client/server system with many branch offices spread about the country, each with a few laser printers. Some applications on the central server produce overnight reports, and the PC applications also have access to these printers via a LAN. For example, the host can print directly to these printers (in which case it would need to know their characteristics, and they would need to be accessible to the host), or the unformatted output can be sent to the client platforms via file transfer, and formatted and printed from there.

Database

The choice of DBMS may also be dictated by what is currently in place in terms of both licensing costs and available skills. If the new system is to use existing databases, then the DBMS is part of the requirement.

The DBMS can be expected to supply access control, data sharing, data consistency through transactions and rollback, data security through backup and rollforward. For client/server it must also provide this functionality through remote access and support management of remote sessions. Ideally, the DBMS will support remote clients transparently, without a significant drop in performance other than that resulting from the remoteness of the client (e.g. communications delays). It should also support those network protocols you are using or are likely to use in the future, again transparently if possible. For example, Oracle's SQL*Net technology allows applications to access local or remote databases transparently over different protocols, accessing different databases on different runs without any code changes.

If distributed databases are to be used, support from the DBMS to maintain them in step is also very useful. If distributed updates are to be done, a two-phase commit protocol may be required. To support distributed functionality, the ability of a DBMS to support stored procedures or user exits may be an important consideration.

It is wise to make use of the in-built DBMS features wherever practical, as writing your own will be both costly and time consuming, and may have to be revisited as DBMS upgrades are taken.

Where different server or client platforms are to be used, the portability of the DBMS and its remote access technology becomes important. The DBMS may be the only commonality between different platforms so it may be appropriate to use the database for communication between functions distributed between client and server. For example, parameters may be passed between functions on the client platform and functions on the server platform through tables in the database, and server functions could be triggered by the setting of data in database tables. Scalability of the DBMS to larger or smaller platforms is also a consideration.

For most client/server applications the DBMS is likely to follow the relational model, with object-oriented databases coming into use as they mature. Other models (network, hierarchical) may be in use by legacy systems, which might not use a DBMS at all (e.g. indexed files).

The type of usage (mostly read, high update transaction volumes, etc.) will help determine the database model used. Other significant factors relating to performance are transaction and data volumes, transaction size, whether queries are *ad hoc* or standard. Some estimation of volumes will be required to support an initial decision on DBMS.

Application design considerations

Transaction cycle and data locking

A DBMS can usually be relied upon to control access to data by many users at a session level, whether those users are on a remote client or on the database server itself. It will ensure database integrity with multiple users or clients reading and writing the same data. However, it will usually expect only one database transaction from each user session at a time (this may or may not be detected or enforced by the DBMS). This restriction could be broken with a multitasking client connected to the database through a single session, acting on data in more than one window at the same time. It may be necessary to build controls into the client application to prevent more than one database transaction being in progress at the same time. A consistent approach to transaction structure has to be enforced within the application.

Locking is used to prevent two or more users updating the same data at the same time, and it is possible to get into a deadlock situation with two users holding one lock, each waiting for the other to give up a lock. There are standard ways of avoiding this (e.g. always lock in the same sequence). With a multitasking client, it is possible for two tasks (windows) to lock each other out, especially as a user can potentially switch around between tasks almost at will.

If locks are held while awaiting user input, the lock could be held for a long time if, for example, the user goes to lunch. However, if a lock is not taken out on data to be updated, it might be changed in the database by some other user while it is being changed on the screen.

An important consideration is the level at which locks are held by the DBMS. This can significantly affect the performance of a system where there may be many clashes between users accessing the same data. If the lock is at the database table level, all other users may be prevented from accessing any data in the table if a lock is held by one user updating one row (although read access might be allowed). If the lock is at the row level, then only those rows required are locked allowing other users access to other rows. Locks may be held at some intermediate level, such as a page, where those pages containing the rows required are locked, blocking access to several rows but leaving those in other pages accessible. While row-level locking can improve performance when many users access the same data, it does introduce an overhead which might slow all transactions, hopefully only imperceptibly.

Maintaining database locks while waiting for user input has implications and disadvantages for the client server design, especially for application servers (i.e. servers which accept requests from client processes to perform business functions which could involve updates to the database):

- The routing mechanism must ensure that all interactions initiated by a specific client must be serviced by the same server as the server is the 'owner' of the database lock.
- If the server should crash, then all the clients associated with that server have to abandon their transactions.
- If the client should crash, or the communications fail, then the server has to be informed so it can rollback that client process's transaction, which clears out locks. This implies a tight linkage between the communications protocol, the operating system, and the server, such as provided by APPC with CICS.
- On client/server systems, it is more likely that transactions will be left incomplete for longer, as users can easily switch from one client process

to another. This leaves the outstanding locks more under the control of the users and can degrade performance. This problem should be designed out by not holding locks or keeping database transactions open over operator input.

There are other strategies, other than database locks, to maintain data integrity. This usually involves the application checking the ownership of the data at update time.

Timestamp the record

When the data is read, a timestamp is recorded either on the record or in a control table, and in the application itself. When the record is about to be updated, the application checks the timestamp to see if it still the same, aborting the transaction if not.

So a timestamp strategy might be:

- Read data and update timestamp in one transaction
- Allow update on screen
- When the user accepts the modifications
- Reread data and check that the timestamp is unchanged; if not, abort the transaction, or else lock the record, update it and then commit the update.

Checking the before image

In cases where other applications update the data using database locks, then the application keeps a copy of the original record and compares it with the database before doing the update, aborting the transaction if different. This can be complex to implement in a generalized way.

With ownership checking, there should be few data clashes if each part of the database is lightly used. Where certain data is heavily used, this approach might result in too many aborted transactions and an alternative would be required, such as software locking.

Software locking

The timestamp mechanism can be enhanced to include a unique session id and status information. Then records, tables or even projects can be reserved by users, and other users prevented from reading for update. A recovery mechanism is required to release locks if a locking user session dies or is disconnected by a network failure. Alternatively, the reservations could have a time limit. Under software locking at row level, users can be informed that data has been reserved, and can then decide their next action, whereas under a database locking regime, they would usually stay 'stuck' until the lock was freed.

Efficient SQL

Techniques for writing efficient SQL are reasonably well documented, and these also apply for client/server. However, there is an additional consideration where SQL is used to communicate between client and server. In order to reduce or eliminate unnecessary network traffic the SQL has to be framed so that the statement is entirely executed on the server. This prevents the transfer of large amounts of data to the client which might subsequently be reduced by clauses of the SQL, or by other SQL statements or procedural code. For example, if data is transferred from table to table it should be done in one SQL statement entirely run on the server, rather than, for example, two SQL statements which transfer data to the client only to be transferred back to the server.

Context-free application servers

Under a traditional transaction cycle which keeps a record locked over user input, the server must maintain the locking context within its data area, and so must have a different data area for each client. In large systems with hundreds of clients, these data areas multiply up and drain system resources. There is the added load in that under a client/server system a user can be running a number of client sessions, each corresponding to a data area within a server.

Both the check at update time and soft-lock strategies allow the possibility of context-free servers. That is, everything you need to know to service the request is either in the message from the client or on the database. The advantages are:

- The server need not be running between interactions.
- The routing to multiple single-thread servers is simplified, as any copy of the server can respond to the client. This also helps load balancing.
- Simplifies server design, as there is no need to remember previous conditions, and no internal state tables (which can easily get very complex). This also simplifies code maintenance and debugging.

Parallelism in the architecture

One of the potential advantages of client/server architecture is the use of 'dead' time – that is, in traditional architectures the user usually has to wait while the computer carries out the previous request. As the client and server each have separate processors, a good architecture should be able to take full advantage of both. If the user can continue with entering the next request while the previous is being processed, the perceived performance is enhanced, and the users can work at their own speed.

There are problems with using such asynchronous requests. The future workflow can be altered by the previous response, and error handling can get complicated if the user has moved on to a new context where repairing the error would be difficult. It is possible for the client task to allow the user to move on, but not to move away from the context of any outstanding requests – for example, not allow the user to start a new transaction until the outstanding transaction update has been serviced.

Fast data entry clerks do not like waiting for the machine at all, and often do not need to know the result of their input immediately. In the above case, with a complex and slow update, consider using a repair queue, where the results of previous transaction updates are received some time later and stored away for later perusal and perhaps repair by the client task.

In OLTP systems with a synchronous messaging system we can make use of background servers. There are some updates which can be performed by a low-priority background task after the on-line server has responded to the client task. For example, although the inventory update for a new order must be immediate, the invoicing can be done later. Such background servers allow the users to continue, even if they have had to wait for the inventory update to complete.

With synchronous messaging systems between client machine and server machine it is still possible to let the user move ahead of the server. Requests could be buffered at the client end of the communications link, and fed to the servers one at a time as the previous reply arrives. Note that this is not significantly different from buffering the request in the mailbox of a single-threaded server. With asynchronous messaging systems the client task must be prepared to receive the reply of a fast request before the reply to a slow request that was sent earlier.

Server management in OLTP systems

Whose responsibility is it to ensure that the requested server is running? For small systems, all the servers can be started at the start of the day and left running. An operator can restart if necessary. OLTP operating systems, such as CICS, or TopEnd for UNIX, take on that responsibility. It is, or should be, one of the responsibilities of client/server middleware. What follows describes the problems and desirable features of server management.

In a large system, running on, say UNIX, or VMS, it is not advisable to have all the servers running, using memory and swap space. Therefore some mechanism must be in place to decide when to stop and start the servers. Apart from the operating system overhead of loading a server from disk, there is the initialization code, and for some database interfaces, the first-time through parsing of embedded SQL Therefore it makes sense not to stop and start servers too often.

Usage parameters for servers could be supplied by a system administrator:

- Do not stop this server
- Do not exceed N users per copy
- Do not allow use of this server at all before midday
- Always have at least N copies running

A more sophisticated mechanism could incorporate the above parameters with a continuous monitoring of server usage, and adjust the number of copies according to queue lengths, CPU usage, or other parameters.

There are two main mechanisms of managing server tasks:

1. *Watching message traffic.* The server manager watches each message and checks if there is a server available to handle it. If not, it either queues the message or starts a server. It also identifies servers that are running but for which there is no demand and may shut them down.
2. *Client registration.* The client tasks registers its desire to use a server and deregisters when it has finished with it. The server management task need only watch for two types of message, and it is clear when to consider closing down a server.

The server management task must also stop and start background servers, probably by monitoring the communication method between on-line server and background server, and starting up servers when some request limit has been exceeded. Server management must also know if an on-line server or background server has crashed and be able to restart it.

A server management task ideally should have read-only access to operating system internals, such as task lists and abort procedures, so that it can easily monitor its servers. These facilities exist to some extent under VMS, and to a much lesser one under UNIX.

OLTP servers as clients

Ideally, a client server system should be built from discrete well-defined business functions, built as APIs. An API should do one simple specialized job for which it can be specially tuned. An application server could then become a series of calls to these self-contained APIs, which are then the reusable building blocks for applications.

The architectural problem is how to implement these APIs. If they are code that is included at link time, then common APIs will be present in all servers, which increases memory requirements. Any change to an API means rebuilding all affected executables. Using shared dynamically loaded libraries will ensure that only one copy of the code is in memory, and effectively uses the operating system to load your APIs for you. This is not possible on some operating systems, especially if you wish to use third-party RDBMS libraries for ESQL, and on others writing code for shared libraries involves technical considerations that stretch the knowledge of normal application programmers, especially around problems of data ownership. Another possibility is to organize these APIs as servers. The application servers then become clients as well.

There are difficulties with this superficially attractive approach. Consider the case where an API was designed to handle all the database access for a single business object. If the API was in-line code, then there could be a read with lock, a check against various conditions on other tables, and then an update of the record. The transaction is committed to the database once all the APIs have completed successfully.

As a server API, a read with lock is one message, with the data returned. The update is another message, with its reply. There are *four* messages. But this method can't work for API servers doing update unless there is a method of implementing two-phase commits. With a two-phase commit, all the updates are performed by the API servers. If the updates are all successful, a message is passed to each server to Prepare-to-commit. This forces the database engine to make all the checks it will need to commit the updates to the database successfully without actually doing it. The database believes that it cannot fail to perform the commit if the Prepare-to-commit succeeds. Once all the Prepare-to-commit messages reply with success, then the commit message itself can be sent to all the servers. So there are now *eight* messages involved for each server API – the read, the update, the Prepare-to-commit, and the commit message, each with its reply – compared to no interprocess communication with linked in code. Also, with a two-phase commit, it is not possible to implement the server APIs as context-free servers.

However, the above complications fade away for enquiry-only server APIs. If they return data that is not to be updated, there is a message and its reply (two messages) and the server can be context-free. As enquiry services tend to be much more in demand by application servers than updates, it is not unreasonable to implement enquiry APIs as servers. If the message interface is designed to be the same as for the application servers, then client tasks could also use these enquiry APIs as if they were simple enquiry application servers.

Building robust OLTP applications

A traditional application program is entitled to stop on an abnormal condition. It only has one user, who can't do anything else anyway, and as long as the user is told of the problem, it reasonable to stop. However, the aim of an OLTP application server is to stay alive. Invalid requests and database errors must be sensibly handled. Error handling and recovery must be very robust, which implies a very thorough regime of testing. All errors should be logged, though if the logging mechanism fails, it is probably right for the server to keep going.

A lot of thought and design should be applied to handling and logging errors, how to quickly climb the calling stack after a deep error, and how to restore the server to handle the next message. During testing, the application servers should be compiled with a debug option that performs extra checks on passed parameters and database values. This should ensure that bugs in function usage and data validity are picked up in an early stage of the development and testing.

A client/server architecture relies on well-defined APIs – between client tasks, networks, business servers and databases. If these APIs are misunderstood or badly used, the components will misbehave. If a message ends with a database error – where has the problem occurred ? Has the client made an incorrect request, the network drivers truncated the message, the incorrect unpacking of the message for the server use, or just a logic error in the SQL? The only way to find out is by an extensive tracking mechanism. The client software must be able to log the requests, the network drivers should be able to log messages, the routers to log all traffic, the servers to log their inputs and their data access requests.

This will, of course, slow down the system enormously, and should only be used as a diagnostic aid in tracking down particular bugs. In practice, it is invaluable to be able to turn logging on and off dynamically for particular client tasks, specified communication routes, and specific servers. It may seem a lot of trouble to go to, but when different development teams produce different components, debugging integration failures will otherwise involve recompilations with display statements, and cause more delays than implementing a flexible logging system.

Different environments

In OLTP systems, there is often the need to have separate development, testing and live environments. This is not as important in EIS systems, as the applications usually run on a workstation or PC, do not usually offer services to other PCs, and do not update the central database.

In OLTP systems, different environments involve having different client tasks, different application servers, and a different database. The communications techniques must be capable of linking a client task to a different set of servers, which are attached to a different database. Moving servers from one environment to another should not involve recompilation or relinking (think of the difficulties at a customer site that would want to test a new release). If there are differences in server behaviour (e.g. attaching to different databases), this information should be read dynamically by the servers from the environment. At the client end, on a PC or workstation, the source directory of the client tasks could be held in the environment, as well as the attach names for network communications.

Designing for different server operating systems

If an OLTP application server (e.g. CICS) is to run on many different operating systems (e.g. VMS, MVS/ESA, OS/2, UNIX, NT) then the architecture and software components must be designed with this in mind. The architecture must be designed to use only the common features – do not expect to use NT Threads or VMS Asynchronous Traps under UNIX. The software must be layered, and the operating system differences hidden from the application programmer. This can be done with a set of APIs, implemented as a library, supplying such services as:

*   Interprocess communications
*   Event notification
*   Shared data access
*   Reading environment variables
*   Printing
*   Spawning new tasks

The application code should be written strictly to standards (e.g. POSIX, ANSI C or ANSI COBOL). The problem here is the use of C or COBOL features that are supported on the development platform but not on the test or target platform. It is not always clear what these features are. It is important to use the compiler switches to indicate or fail non-POSIX code on compilation, and to keep a list of coding constructs that cause trouble.

The complete system will also include various operator scripts, and these must also be ported to all platforms. This is more complex, as there isn't as yet an agreed and commonly implemented POSIX command line script language. VMS DCL is not UNIX scripts!

Different databases in an OLTP environment

If designing application servers with embedded SQL (ESQL), then be aware that it will not be easy to port to a different RDBMS. There is not as yet an agreed standard for ESQL across database suppliers. The standard that is emerging for ESQL is a primitive lowest common denominator. As most of the ESQL vendors supply high-level functions and constructs, it would be a large undertaking to make code that was automatically portable to a different database.

Summary

Client/server design doesn't in itself introduce many new issues to the logical design of systems, rather, it brings together the issues associated with distributed computing, GUIs, open systems, relational databases, right-sizing, and interworking of components from different vendors. It is often possible to build a client/server system using or upgrading existing components, such as PCs, networks, databases and even existing applications.

The most far-reaching decision about new client/server implementations is where to place the application logic. Usually it is clear that the presentation will take place on the client platform, and most, if not all, of the database component will reside on a server platform. But where to place the application logic? Should it run on the client platform, near the presentation, or on the server, near the database? We have assumed earlier in this chapter that for EIS systems, the application resides with presentation [PA] ~ [D], and for OLTP, the bulk of the application resides near the database [P] ~ [AD]. Lets look at the pros and cons of each location.

Application on client platform

For

- For EIS systems, the application is largely concerned with presentation and formatting of the data, and so should reside with the presentation.
- RDBMS vendors usually supply a connection method for remote access to their database, so connectivity can usually be easily provided by third-party middleware.
- If the application uses the CPU intensively (e.g. a complex iterative recalculation), it may be advantageous only to slow down the requester on his or her own CPU, rather than the central CPU used by everybody.
- Applications running under a MS-Windows style interface can take advantage of DDE, OLE, Cut & Paste to interact with other applications.

Against

- If SQL is used as the communications technique, then the application must use SQL that allows the DBMS to do most, if not all, of the selection. Heavy network loading and reduced responses would result if the application had to sift through a large number of records to extract a useful subset.
- Note that OLTP database updates will often involve checking the data integrity against other tables, interspersed with program logic. This could involve many SQL statements, each involving network traffic.

Application on server platform

For

- Complex program logic has direct and fast access to the data.

- If the application resides on a different processor from the presentation, then the user need not held up by the application. Simultaneous processing can take place, making the system feel more responsive.
- Applications can take advantage of common modules and object-oriented methods more easily if the application components are centralized.
- Applications can stay resident, and thus only incur a single initialization overhead. Some ESQL involves an expensive parsing process that slows down processing when the SQL statements are first processed. Therefore keeping an application server alive for further requests will also speed up the SQL access.
- Applications can more easily take advantage of server system resources, such as bulk printing or interfacing to other systems. Also, background processes can more easily interact with on-line applications.
- Easier to upgrade to new versions of the application software for large systems.

Against

- Communication between the client platform and the application is often more complex to implement.

From the above, it is most likely that EIS style systems will place the application on the client platform, and OLTP-based systems would most likely prefer the application near the database.

EIS is easier to implement

Third-party vendors have concentrated in this area of the market, and can provide a range of data-presentation products off the shelf. They will usually allow a connection to remote databases via middleware supplied by the major database vendors.

OLTP application servers are more complex

The following issues get more difficult to resolve if the applications and database(s) reside on a network of server platforms. The best approach in such circumstances is to look for a middleware product that can handle these complexities:

- The connection between the client platform and the application servers
- Stopping and starting the server applications
- Server location transparency

Other OLTP issues

- You will most likely want an application server to handle requests from many client processes, as this leads to single rather than multiple initialization overheads, and better use of server platform resources.
- Consider using context-free servers.
- Consider using a data-integrity method that does not involve data locking for long periods, such as timestamping or software locking.
- When considering using servers as clients, try to avoid multiple updates across servers, as the implied two-phase commit adds complexity and extra data traffic.
- Consider an architecture that fully utilizes the client and server CPUs, and at least allows the user to type ahead.
- Remember that application servers must be more robust than ordinary programs, and so there must be strict testing and a sophisticated debugging and logging environment.
- If the application servers must port to a number of platforms, be sure the architecture uses the lowest common denominator of system services.
- Porting to different RDBMSs is more difficult than it would at first appear.

For both EIS and OLTP systems, remember:

- Inefficient SQL is a major source of poor performance.
- Don't forget issues about printing and routing reports to personal printers.
- Be sure to understand the limitations as well as the benefits of any middleware products.

4 Connectivity

We are discussing in this chapter the link that connects the client platform with the server platform. Of particular interest is what goes on at the higher levels of the ISO seven-layer model, rather than the lower (Figure 4.1).

There is some scope for confusion here between the user presentation, which is a major focus for client/server systems and the OSI Presentation layer, which 'presents' the session layer to the application. Most of what we are discussing in this book takes place at the Application level of the OSI model, and we assume that a suitable telecommunications network to provide the lower layers is in place, or can be built, based on one of the standard protocol stacks, such as TCP/IP or SNA or a combination, linked by a gateway mechanism.

This is not to say that this lower-level infrastructure is trivial or irrelevant, but merely a reflection that the telecommunications world has reached a level of maturity where a designer may take for granted that a robust network can be built. It is also true that the distinction between

Application	7
Presentation	6
Session	5
Transport	4
Network	3
Logical link	2
Physical	1

Figure 4.1
Seven-layer communications model.

WANs, LANs and even computer channels is blurring: they may all be made out of fiber-optical technology, they can all go at 100Mb/s, and they can all stretch over land, sea or sky with ease.

Speed does still come at a price (see Chapter 6) but the difference is declining. With such services as ATM on the near horizon, designers can increasingly assume 100Mb/s as a base.

All the above is valid in Western Europe and the USA, for example, but is not so in many other parts of the world. If designers are working in those less fortunate areas, the level of telecommunications available will have a decisive influence on the design of their systems. Interestingly, that may be to promote the use of client/server techniques: when considering the provision of airline departure control systems in Russia, for example, the lack of reliable telecommunications ruled out a totally centralized system, such as is typical of Western airlines, and led to a design with more local intelligence at airports. Passenger lists from the central reservations system would be updated when the link became available. Other than this brief discussion we do not plan to spend time on the lower layers.

Network implications

In Chapter 3 we have defined six ways in which a client/server system may be built, depending on the point at which the split between client and server is defined. According to the choice, the traffic across the link will differ in several important ways. First, the volume, second, the pattern and third, the relevant international standards will differ.

Let us consider the simple example of the workstation and the relational database server handling an order entry application. We want the application to check the customer's status as well as the product's availability before accepting the order.

If the database server provides strict adherence to the current ANSI SQL standard, no more and no less, we know that the client will be sending SQL strings to the server and the server will send data and return codes back again. We thus have presentation and application on the workstation, and the database on the server ([PA]~[D]). This has some attractions, not least that the traffic across the link is well defined. In our example, there would be three request/result pairs – one for the customer status, one for the product availability and, hopefully, one to register the order. Note that a lot of avoidable traffic will be carried across the link. Each transaction (which may be repeated thousands of times every hour) will have to have its full SQL syntax sent across the link.

The SQL for checking the customer and the product and for updating the order table could, however, be stored on the database machine as a macro or 'stored procedure'. Order entry would then still involve the same three transactions, but each transmission would be much smaller than before. We would thus have shifted a component of the application logic onto the server ([PA]~[AD]).

The next step along this path would be to move the rest of the application logic onto the database server, so that it handles the entire transaction ([P]~[AD]). This will require one single request/result pair, with the result being merely a return code – a considerable reduction in network traffic. In other words, we could handle the business transaction in three different ways, all valid, but all showing considerably different loadings on the network.

The three different ways also have different levels of adherence to international standards: the first, which only sends ANSI SQL across the network is the purest. The second, using extensions to SQL which are not defined by standards, is likely to be proprietary to the database vendor. The third could be implemented in two basic ways: using either a vendor-supplied package to handle the client/server link (proprietary) or a TP monitor which complies with the X-Open standards (open). Both of these would come under the heading of 'middleware', which we discuss later.

Adherence to standards may or may not be important: but certainly if future flexibility is desired, it is probably to be valued. In the first case, where only pure ANSI SQL is sent across the network, one would be confident of being able to replace the server's hardware and software if the need arose. Equally, by using a TP monitor which adheres to the X-Open standards, one may have some confidence in one's ability to switch components.

In the proprietary cases, one's ability to switch would be determined by the supplier of the communications mechanism. This is not necessarily too limiting, since most vendors find it necessary to port their products to most of the major hardware platforms. It goes to show that the old dilemma about choosing genuinely open versus proprietary solutions is still very much alive: only the ground has shifted.

We have so far identified three communication mechanisms: SQL, stored procedures and 'process to process'. To these we should add 'store and forward', 'file transfer' and, perhaps futuristically, 'object–object'. A fairly complete list is as follows.

Terminal emulation

There are many software packages which will exploit the power of the workstation to make it emulate a 'dumb' terminal, at least in its appearance to the server. Many are also quite clever at reformatting screen layouts to present a modern, GUI appearance to the user, if required.

Communication is obviously at the level of presentational control, with the screen appearance and user actions being transferred. This could be character by character (e.g. ASCII), page mode (e.g. 3270) or graphical object (e.g. X-Windows). A single-user transaction will result in many, probably small, communications. The connection could be made via a LAN or through a direct terminal connection.

File transfer

Communication is achieved by passing files between client and server. Files can contain whatever form of data needs to be transferred. They may need to be translated (e.g. ASCII/EBCDIC) or reformatted by client or server. The file transfer protocols of the lower layers are used to move the files using fast block-mode transfers, and these may provide some form of atomic transaction, guaranteeing that a file is either fully transferred or not at all with some built-in error detection and correction.

File redirection

Communication is again via a file mechanism, but by directly accessing the file on a remote platform through a network file system (e.g. Novell or NFS). There may or may not be any form of atomic transaction or error correction provided by the redirector.

Process to process (object to object)

There are many forms of process to process communication, but they will generally fall into the categories of asynchronous (e.g. message passing) or synchronous (e.g. remote procedure call RPC). One type can be converted into the other by additional software layers. There may be some queuing provided, allowing senders to send while receivers are busy, and receivers to wait when no senders are ready. There may be support for multiple senders and/or receivers.

Process to process is theoretically the most flexible method as a specific interface can be defined to meet whatever requirements exists. Communication traffic will be greatly affected by this choice. However, if a truly custom solution is built, it will require much more programming effort, including that of ensuring the ACID properties discussed later. An alternative is to use a TP monitor to provide standard programming interfaces, the ACID properties and the communications links.

Some authorities believe that objects point the way ahead, and standards are being developed to cover the passing of messages between objects. Most vaunted among these is CORBA, the Common Object Request Broker Architecture, as put forward by the Object Management Group, a consortium of software and hardware vendors.

Message queues (store and forward)

With message queues, communication is again provided on a process-to-process basis, but with longer-lasting queues. Each process will typically remove a transaction from a queue, process it and return it to another queue for further processing. Queues will be saved to non-volatile storage so that they are not lost. A message queue mechanism is most useful for asynchronous communications, where a process needs to be carried out, but not necessarily in real time.

SQL

Communication takes place through SQL statements, either transferring source text from client to server or converting the text into lower-level units. Results are returned by the server. Atomic transactions are provided by the server's DBMS. The communication protocol is likely to be proprietary, but the interface to the client is likely to be published and supported by third parties. This mechanism is favoured by EIS systems, in which the SQL is generated on a workstation, the search carried out on the database machine and the results returned to the workstation for display.

Stored procedures

Here the client transmits triggers to the server where the DBMS executes stored procedures to deliver results. The communication can be reduced compared with an SQL level interface, as only the name of the procedure to be run, and any run-time parameters need to be communicated, not the whole procedure itself. This method is particularly useful where the same procedures will be run over and over again. The DBMS will provide the atomic transactions.

The above list may be mapped quite easily onto the six example architectures discussed in Chapter 3, and the following combinations of component connectivity can be derived. In each case one or more particular types of connection are suitable.

Presentation to presentation P~P

The connection is almost certainly a terminal protocol such as 3270 or VT100.

Presentation to application P~A

The connection is also likely to be a terminal protocol (albeit at a higher level) such as X-Windows.

Application to database A~D

This connection is likely to be at SQL level if communicating to a DBMS, or through a network file redirector if communicating to a network file server. It is likely to be proprietary to the DBMS vendor.

Application to database (with stored procedures) A~AD

The connection here may be a combination of SQL which implicitly triggers stored procedures and explicit triggers. It is likely to be proprietary to the DBMS vendor.

Application to application A~A

This connection will be some form of process-to-process communication method, which may be proprietary or open. It could take the form of message passing or remote procedure calls, for example.

Whichever of the above mechanisms are chosen, its implementation can usually be greatly eased by the use of vendor packages, generically called 'middleware'. These handle many of the intricacies of dealing with the network, and of providing such facilities as message handling and security.

Middleware

Middleware provides a software layer that protects the application from the underlying infrastructure, such as network communications, and may be loosely grouped into three categories:

1. *Distributed computing.* This provides the facilities that allow client and server processes to cooperate over a distributed network of machines. OSF's DCE is an example of this type.
2. *Database access.* This offers SQL and ESQL services to applications, and allows connections to remote RDBMSs – for example, Oracle's SQL*Net.
3. *On-line transaction processing (OLTP) monitors.* These provide transaction integrity by offering commit and rollback facilities for transactions that may be nested, and may involve resources spread across more than one machine. They hide the communications altogether and provide simple APIs. In the UNIX world, products such as TOP END provides such facilities.

Ideally, middleware itself should be layered, such that database and OLTP middleware would sit on top of a standard distributed computing middleware. A good example of this is Encina, an OLTP product, that sits on DCE. Currently, most OLTP and database middleware products use their own mechanisms for handling the complexity of distributed computing, although standards are emerging in this area. We will examine these three groups in more detail.

Distributed computing

A distributed computing environment is especially useful where there are many networked host machines. The type of facilities they can offer are:

- *Distributed file systems*. Files and printers can be made visible to all server and client platforms.
- *Location transparency and naming services*. The client process need not be aware of where the server process resides. The server process could even be moved from one platform or software partition to another, and still be transparently available to the caller. All resources should be available by name only, and a naming service then converts the name to the correct format for the underlying operating system.
- *Data conversion*. The middleware should perform any ASCII-to-EBCDIC conversions. Also, as different environments represent data in different ways, (e.g. integers are held in different ways on different platforms) some conversion must be supplied by the middleware. This is usually performed using a Remote Procedure Call (RPC) interface, with eXternal Data Representation (XDR) technology.
- *Server management*. The middleware should be aware of server requests, and so stop and start the servers as required, using some defined administration policy. Load balancing and auto-restart after server crashes are also useful.
- *Security*. Should this client process be allowed to communicate with this server process or use this printer? Client identification and access rights should be controlled by the middleware. Auditing of accesses can be useful for security and for performance monitoring.
- *Time services*. The middleware should ensure that the time is synchronized across all the platforms. This is crucial for timestamping mechanisms.
- *Administration services*. These include facilities to monitor the status and performance of the system, manage the introduction of software upgrades and allow some dynamic reconfiguration.

In order to take advantage of these facilities, across equipment from several vendors, there must be agreed standards. The great hope in this area seems to be based on the OSF DCE model, which apparently has the backing of the major vendors. It remains to be seen how quickly real function is delivered, however, and until such time as it is, the concept of freely interconnected heterogeneous platforms remains just that, a concept.

Database access

This class of middleware varies considerably in sophistication. At its simplest, it could supply a method to connect a set of workstations to a single remote database. The most complex are those that offer the application a virtual or logical database, which physically comprises a variety of different data types and vendor platforms. An interface is provided to allow users to access this database directly.

There are attempts to introduce standards in this area, by extending the current SQL standards to include macros and triggers. There are also attempts by vendors to establish their product APIs as the *de facto* standards – ODBC is an example here. While standards are not agreed, it is always wise to be careful about committing one's company to an interface which may prove transient. It should always be done consciously and not accidentally.

Some corporate databases are scattered over many machines, possibly supplied by many database vendors. In order to access this data, the applications ideally should not concern themselves with which data is stored where and in what specialized format. A 'virtual database' presents this distributed database as a single entity. The middleware contains mapping and conversion information to enable access across different database tables, views and formats.

At its simplest, the virtual database could present different tables from different databases but supplied by the same vendor running on the same machine – such as two Oracle databases on one UNIX platform. At its most complex, tables could be split across databases supplied by different vendors running on different platforms. In a multivendor virtual database there is always the problem that there is not as yet a standard for the high-level SQL constructs, so either the virtual database will have do sophisticated conversions or it will fail on all but the simplest of constructs.

The virtual database is difficult to implement, and usually involves a lot of network traffic and data conversion. There are difficult problems to resolve if the applications attempt updates across heterogeneous databases. This, in turn, implies that the application designer needs to know which data is not distributed. The virtual database is most useful in EIS systems, where the data is more likely to be distributed, updates can be restricted and response times are not critical.

The obvious alternative to the virtual database is the real database, or data warehouse in which data is copied from operational systems into a EIS database designed for the purpose. The connection between this and the workstation can be relatively straightforward, but the penalty is the cost of copying and duplicating the data. The environment offered on the workstation can also vary from the simple to the highly complex (for example, from a spreadsheet macro to an application development environment).

This class of middleware is probably the most popular, and is available from database vendors, workstation tool vendors and software houses. It offers the ability to construct application systems quickly (using the power of the workstation combined with that of a relational DBMS). Its drawback is that the protocols employed are almost bound to be proprietary in some degree, which may effectively 'lock in' a user to that vendor for the future.

OLTP middleware (also known as transaction processing (TP) monitors or managers)

Early transaction processing (TP) monitors, such as CICS, grew directly out of teleprocessing, that exciting development when computers were first linked to terminals by telephone lines. It quickly became clear that handling a stream of small requests from users sitting at terminals required management that was radically different from that provided by the standard operating systems, which were primarily aimed at batch processing. For one thing, telephone lines were notoriously unreliable, which meant that error handling had to be very sophisticated. For another, the overhead of starting up a new operating system task was (and still is) very high and out of proportion to the nature of a single transaction: that meant that TP monitors had to provide their own task-management capabilities, including the isolation of each transaction from every other transaction running in the system.

In addition, programming for TP tasks was rather complex, since it involved dealing with telecommunications. Another function of the TP monitor therefore became the provision of a simple programming interface which allowed the programmer to forget all these complexities and simply code the business logic requirements.

In summary, the early TP monitors provided extensions to the operating system, an API and a series of functions in support of what are now known as the ACID properties of a transaction: Atomicity, Consistency, Isolation and Durability. Atomicity means that each transaction may be treated as an entity, complete in itself, and will not leave the database with some tables updated when others have failed. Consistency means ensuring that the system moves from one consistent state to another with each transaction. Isolation is the property of keeping each transaction entirely separate from others (even though many transactions may be handled concurrently). Durability means ensuring that a transaction, once committed, is never lost.

With the passage of time, many of the extensions to the operating system have been provided either by the operating system or by other layers of code: for example, the network is now handled by specialized software which provides services to the TP monitor. With the arrival of self-contained RDBMS software, the TP monitor need not concern itself with database issues. Indeed, some RDBMS vendors believe quite sincerely that TP monitors are not required at all, since their software provides all the data integrity one could wish.

Moreover, with the arrival of intelligent client systems the problem of context is relieved. The problem is as follows. A business transaction often requires several computer transactions, as in the case of order processing in which the customer's status and the product stock level must be checked before placing the order on the system. During this sequence of computer transactions some working data such as the customer number must be held over from one transaction to the next. In the days of centralized computers supporting 'dumb' terminals this could only be done on the central system, and was handled by the TP monitor, which would provide the programmer with a scratch-pad area on demand. Into this area would be written the 'context' data, such as the customer number. This effectively means that the entire string of transactions for one user must be handled by the same processor, because the scratch-pad area is attached to that processor. This in turn limits the possibility of using distributed or parallel computer systems.

With the advent of the client workstation, with its own processing capability, context data may be stored there, rather than at the central server. This relieves the server of having to 'context switch' when dealing with transactions from more than user. Transactions can now be more freely distributed across multiple engines on the server.

However, additional complexities have arisen in the form of distributed systems and multiple database vendors. Furthermore, it's not just databases that are involved in business transactions: it may be that a ticket needs to be printed, or a fax sent as part of a business transaction. TP monitors are thus evolving into generalized transaction managers, which operate across distributed systems and provide a high-level mechanism for communication.

The X-Open committee has devised a standard model for transaction management, which is represented in Figure 4.2. This defines an interface (called XA) to resource managers of any description, although database managers are the most obvious candidates. This interface includes verbs such as COMMIT and ROLLBACK, which are used to signal the successful conclusion of a transaction, or the need to unwind it, restoring the system to its previous consistent state. The XA interface also specifies the more complex 'two-phase commit' process, which is used to manage transactions which involve changing the state of two or more separate entities, such as two different databases.

Two-phase commit improves the chances of surviving problems within a distributed system, but only at the price of a significant increase in traffic

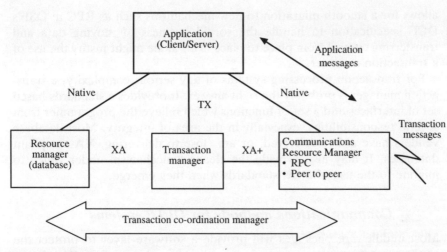

Figure 4.2
Distributed
transaction processing
model.

between the TP manager and the resource managers. Two-phase commit must be used with care, as it can have considerable impact on the performance and cost of a system. It is easy to design client/server systems which depend on two-phase commit, because they are by their nature distributed, and distributed resources are exactly those which will need it.

The XA interface is used by the Transaction Manager, rather than the application, which invokes the Transaction Manager to handle resources, using the TX interface. The benefit of doing this is precisely to relieve the programmer from worrying about transaction integrity. The programmer defines the beginning and the end of a transaction, and the transaction manager takes responsibility for its integrity.

Of course, the application may bypass the transaction manager if it chooses, and use the Native (for which read proprietary) interfaces to the resource managers. The protection offered by the transaction manager and the standards-based interface are thus relinquished. This is defensible in simple MIS systems, for example.

Note that the X-Open model of transactions does not specify where the process begins: it may be that the transaction manager calls the application or that the application calls the transaction manager. The former case is the one most widely in use today for handling routine business transactions, but any application process which needs the services of a transaction manager can have them, simply by identifying the start and end points of the transaction, and by using the transaction manager to handle resources. In this way, an application can forget the details of handling unsuccessful transactions – the transaction manager will ensure that every transaction is either successfully completed or that the system is restored to its previous state.

Note also that the X-Open model recognizes the special place of telecommunications managers in distributed transaction processing, and allows for a smooth migration to new mechanisms such as RPC in OSF's DCE specification to handle the sordid business of moving data and transferring control from place to place. This alone might justify the use of a transaction manager.

For transaction processing systems of any serious complexity, a transaction manager is probably the right answer. It provides a standards-based set of interfaces and a set of functions which relieve the programmer from several responsibilities, especially in the area of integrity. Most database vendors have either delivered, or are close to delivering, XA-compliant databases. It may also provide the cleanest mechanism under which to migrate to the use of DCE standards when they emerge.

Communications methods for OLTP systems

Most middleware packages will provide a software layer to protect the applications from the complexities outlined in this section. The issues raised here will be of interest to those concerned with the internals of communications techniques, especially as they relate to server management (i.e. stopping and starting servers).

If a server could receive all its incoming requests through the same communication channel, this would simplify the architecture, as the server only has to wait on one event – the arrival of a message. As many clients can usually talk to one server, a many-to-one communication technique would be the most appropriate. The reply address would need to included in the request message itself. The ability for more than one copy of a server to be waiting on a single communication channel is also an advantage for context-free servers, as the load can easily be spread. Most network communications do not support either of these features, with the exception of named pipes under LAN Server, LAN Manager or Netware for OS/2, which supply a many-to-one concept.

The communication methods employed depend to a large extent on how the routing of the messages is to be performed. If the client talks directly to the server, it has to know its location and its access name. The server also has to be running and implementing a server management system as described above becomes impossible. Also it becomes difficult to reconfigure the servers, as all the client tasks have somehow to be informed.

Most modern complex client/server systems pride themselves on location transparency – that is, the client task does not need to know where the server is located. This is implemented by sending requests to some form of name server or router, which is responsible of matching the service name to a particular server task, locating where it resides and ensuring that it is running. It then sends on the request.

If in practice all the servers are on the same machine as the router, then it is tempting to use interprocess communication techniques between the router and the servers, as these techniques are usually faster and more

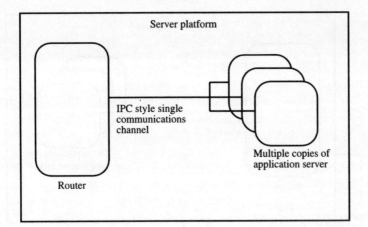

Server platform

IPC style single
communications
channel

Multiple copies of
application server

Router

Figure 4.3
Shared memory
system.

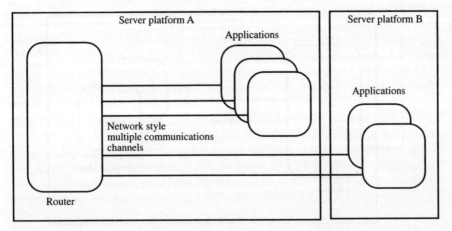

Server platform A

Applications

Server platform B

Applications

Network style
multiple communications
channels

Router

Figure 4.4
Central routing
system.

flexible than network communications. Some techniques are memory based, also provide a many-to-one concept, and more than one process can wait on the data, allowing a trivial mechanism for load balancing multiple copies of servers. In the case of building a turnkey system this could be acceptable, but for a generalized client/server architecture for a corporate environment, such inflexibility of server location would amount to a design flaw (see Figure 4.3).

There are two ways of overcoming this limitation. First, the router uses a network communications technique, regardless of whether the server is local or on another machine (Figure 4.4). This simplifies the communications problem, but may impose a processing overhead for local communications. Also, the problem of server management of tasks on different machines becomes difficult.

Figure 4.5
Distributed routing
system.

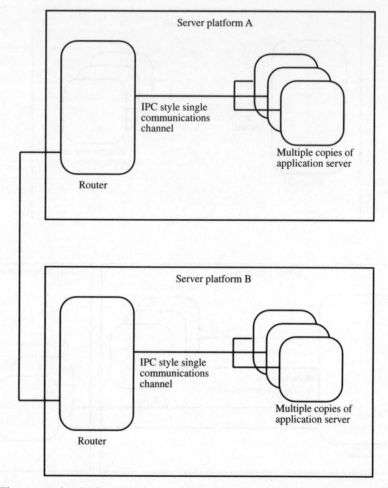

The second solution involves a router on each machine, which talks to other routers using network communications, and its own servers using interprocess communications. Once a name server has located the machine with the application server, it passes the responsibility for the conversation to the router on that machine (Figure 4.5).

Within the UNIX world, TCP/IP sockets is the *de facto* standard for peer-to-peer communications across different machines. Sockets provides a simple read/write interface, and a two-way channel (i.e. allows duplex communications). One end, usually a server, would listen for incoming requests for conversations, and can have many conversations running simultaneously. Blocked and unblocked reads are available, and a process can wait for input on many conversations simultaneously. There are many implementations of sockets for PCs and workstations. VMS also can provide sockets support. Sockets do not have a many-to-one concept – each conversation involves a single end-to-end connection.

Within the IBM world, APPC/APPN provides peer-to-peer communications. This is a half-duplex protocol, so two conversations are required for full-duplex operation. APPC is a complex protocol, and the implementors of both ends usually have to agree what features to support before coding commences. The advantage of APPC is that implementations of it usually provide a mechanism to start a transaction process automatically when a connection request is made. Also, as APPC is built into VTAM operating system, communication errors or disconnections can be used to abort associated tasks. This takes on some of the responsibilities of a server management system.

Within an OS/2 network, TCP/IP and APPC are supported. Named pipes are also supported, which can be used to implement a many-to-one construct, which is useful to client/server. The current implementation has the unfortunate limitation that pipes can only be created on the machine on which the LAN Server software resides, so if a client can also be a server, you can't use named pipes.

Summary

- Client/server design is primarily concerned with the top two levels of the OSI model.
- Lower-level connectivity can and should be hidden by middleware and communications software.
- The form of connection between components is chosen depending on such factors as:
  - Communications infrastructure
  - Support for standards
  - Components to be connected
  - Performance requirements
  - Type of business transactions
- Use of middleware to provide this connectivity is recommended over a custom-building approach.
- Standards are still emerging in this area – be careful.

5 Migration and coexistence

A most important element of any plan to incorporate client/server technology into an existing computer environment addresses the problems of coexistence between the old and the new. In a few cases, there may be an opportunity for a clean break, but generally the incorporation of client/server capability will be gradual. This is almost certainly the right policy, since client/server technology is still new, still raises system management issues which may not be readily soluble, and will almost certainly bring more benefits in some areas than others.

Phase 1 – The data warehouse

Identifying a start point should not be too difficult. One area in which this technology has proved itself, is in the analysis of data already collected by 'production' systems. A very common frustration of existing managers is that they are aware that data they could use is held on computer disks but they have no access to it. This has led to such concepts as the 'data warehouse', which tackles this issue directly by the building of a central repository of production data, usually in relational form, with easy access for any (authorized) users. The data warehouse may be a new physical database, created from copies of production data, or it may be a logical entity, created by a layer of software providing simple access routes to the existing data (Figure 5.1).

Marketing departments are often highly frustrated by an inability to access the customer database, making their efforts to increase sales to existing customers more difficult, and equally tarnishing the company's image by sending out inappropriate mailshots. Ask yourself how often your bank has invited you to take out a student loan even though you are not a student, or a mortgage, even though you already have one with them. General management can also be frustrated by the same lack of access to existing data, which could help them run the company more efficiently, spot trends, identify problem areas and so forth.

Figure 5.1
The data warehouse.

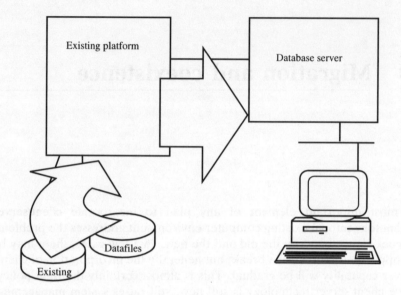

This is fertile territory for a first step into client/server technology: it brings immediate benefit and the risks are low. Such systems are not critical to the day-to-day running of the company, so do not need disaster-recovery plans or high service levels. It is usually possible to identify a small department or group of people who could make profitable use of such a capability, which will keep the costs low. Ideally, these people should be willing to 'have a go', either because they naturally so disposed or because they are sufficiently motivated by the opportunities.

The project plan to provide this facility will need to embrace the following steps, not necessarily handled in this order:

1. What PC hardware and software will the users have? Err on the side of generosity with the hardware, and look for stable, well-supported software.
2. How will they be connected to the server (the physical embodiment of the data warehouse)? A simple LAN connection will probably be best. Err on the side of high speeds.
3. What data is needed, how much of it is there, where is it now, and how will I move it onto the new server?
4. What will the server hardware be? This will depend on the existing set-up: spare capacity on an existing system will be tempting, but a dedicated system is definitely preferable. Ensure that the system can be readily upgraded to five times the initial power. Buy from a reputable supplier and ensure that hardware and operating system maintenance is available. Parallel hardware design is definitely beneficial in this kind of system, especially as data volumes grow.

5. What will the server software be? At heart, it will be a relational database manager. It must be able to grow into a full data warehouse, so it must handle this initial system with contemptuous ease. It must have good data loading facilities and good support. There is a small number of products which meet these criteria. The server must also be supported by the products chosen for the client workstations. Insist on seeing the two working together before buying. Many database software companies will suggest that you buy their workstation tools as well, but beware of becoming totally 'locked in'. Half the point of all this is that you should be able to change or add new tools, or change the server if necessary.

6. How will the users be trained? This is very important and must be done thoroughly. The users will also need a helpdesk of some sort when they get started. This will take at least two full-time staff. They should not only respond to problems but also compile a 'newsletter' containing hints and tips, things to avoid, new facilities to try.

7. How will the system be supported? Who will resolve hardware and software problems? Telecomms issues? It is important for user morale that problems are dealt with professionally from day 1. It is also on day 1 that many problems will appear, so it is important to have the problem-solving mechanism well oiled before that date.

8. Who is going to pay for all this? This is a vital question in most organizations. The budget may not be large by comparison with existing IT expenditure, but it will not be trivial either. Also, it is unfair to expect the initial user department to bear all the 'set-up' costs. If you cannot get enthusiastic funding and support from senior management, consider abandoning the project.

9. How will I measure the benefits? Costs are all too clear, but benefits often less so. It is important to have as clearly stated as possible what are the major gains envisaged and, if possible, what their value to the organization is.

This project should be run on aggressive timescales. If it can't be done within 6 months, start again. Reduce the scale, be less ambitious, or rethink your timings. It is perfectly possible to spend months and months in selecting hardware and software, and good fun it can be! However, technology is moving at such a pace in these areas that new hardware and software is probably appearing faster than you can evaluate it. Consider using an experienced outsider to cut the times.

If you can't decide between two possibilities on technical merit, cost, support or other obvious criteria – toss a coin. It is probably more important to get started than to evaluate any further – remember that you are looking for a system that will handle this initial project 'with contemptuous ease'.

Existing IT departments may not have the right people to run this project. They have grown used to timescales that are lengthy – they probably cannot conceive of this project being complete within 6 months, but it should be. A major benefit of this technology is that it can deliver function fast – this needs to be demonstrated.

With a following wind, you should have a small set of trained users sitting in front of their new workstations very quickly, and they will have ready access to the data they always craved. There is a saying that when God wishes to punish us, he gives us what we want! This is often true of such users – they will discover that this data is not as clear, clean and simple as they imagined. They will find that the same customer appears several times with slightly different addresses, that the meaning of the word 'customer' needs careful definition, that people lead complicated private lives, that private customers are often business customers, too, and it isn't always easy to spot.

This, however, is a *good thing!* The result of this learning process is a beneficial flow of demands for the data to be cleaned up, which, although irritating, is ultimately to the good of the whole organization. Sometimes this clean-up is achieved as part of the loading process – when data comes out of production systems it can be scanned for errors and omissions and corrective action taken. It also results in a set of users who thoroughly understand the data they are working with.

The result of this initial project – which is Phase 1 of the migration process – will range from complete, euphoric success to dismal failure. If the latter is the case, the reasons need to be identified. If the conclusion is that 'client/server technology is not for us' it will be a great pity. More likely, the project was unsuitable, the users coerced, the training or funding inadequate.

Euphoric success is probably the worst outcome! That would lead to more and more users demanding more and more access to more and more data, and an inevitable decline from that heady point.

Most likely, some aspects of the project will have been successful, some areas will have been shown to be inadequate, but hopefully the users will at least have glimpsed how different things might be and will be on the side of progress. Sometimes that glimpse is a real eye-opener – and users become evangelists, committed to the benefits that such a system could offer. Sometimes they conclude that a data specialist working alongside them would be the best way to operate; this is often true of senior executives who don't have the time (or perhaps the aptitude) for 'data mining', but can certainly make use of good information.

Most certainly, lessons will have been learned about the new technology used, the communications links, the hardware, the software, the support and the organization will have gained some firm foundations on which to build. So much for Phase 1.

Phase 2 – Growth and migration

Phase 2 is about growth from this humble beginning, which may happen in three different ways:

1. The existing users will want the system improved with more data, better tools, and so forth
2. Other users will see the potential benefits in their areas and will want access
3. This is the first migration from the existing systems.

We shall concentrate on the last of these, pausing only to note that items 1 and 2 not only require simple growth but will also need the installation of system management processes as certain thresholds are crossed.

Item 3 is of interest in that it addresses the issue of migrating applications from the 'legacy' system. By providing direct access to data for users, the need for regular printed reports from operational systems will decline. Perhaps whole sections of an existing system which provided those reports can be discontinued. Note we are not migrating the whole application, only the reporting programs. This provides benefit in two ways: first, it relieves the processing load on existing systems a little and second, it relieves the maintenance load. Interestingly, it is often the reporting systems that generate the bulk of maintenance requests in traditional systems, so savings in the application development department can be significant.

These initial savings will point the way for other similar savings which may provide enough justification on their own for the provision of workstations to other departments. These departments obtain not only the information they previously had but also access to new information and the ability to tailor reports easily and in their own time. In this way, load from existing hardware can be removed, perhaps enough to defer that next expensive upgrade.

All three parts of Phase 2, the growth phase, will run forever, or at least until the 'data warehouse' way of doing business has become the norm. Also, an organization may stop at this point: it will be getting value out of client/server technology and off-loading its production systems. Even so, it will find itself upgrading its server hardware and its telecommunications links and, most importantly, having to face up to the system management issues discussed earlier. It is possible to upgrade the software on six workstations one Saturday afternoon: upgrading sixty is a different job entirely. More likely, however, it will move to Phases 3 or 4 or both.

Phase 3 – New applications

In Phase 3 new production applications are developed which are significantly different in character from the previous generation. They are built in the knowledge that they must feed the data warehouse as the primary way of informing the organization. This focuses attention on data integrity issues above all else, and, of course, eliminates the need to specify report formats, which often account for a large proportion of system specifications. In addition, the users are more informed about computer systems, and about the data they collect, so they can be more helpful about what is needed. This will reduce the time both to specify and to build the new application.

New applications will also be built based directly on the data warehouse: for example, the running of mailshot campaigns uses data in the warehouse not only to establish the target for a given mailshot but will also store customer reactions back into the warehouse for subsequent analysis.

Finally, users will develop an increasing ability to use existing data on their workstations in new and creative ways to meet demands that would previously have necessitated a piece of software development.

Phase 4 – Further migration

Phase 4 consists of the direct migration of existing applications from the 'old' computer systems to the world of client/server. We have already seen that much of the reporting within the old systems will migrate easily to the new platform, but what remains is a core of production systems which may be dealt with in one of two ways:

1. Rewrite or otherwise migrate to the client/server platform
2. Decide to leave forever on the 'old' platform

Strong candidates for method 2 are those which are going to die naturally over time. There is little point expending effort for a short remaining life. Examples here are systems which support a range of products which are no longer sold. Similarly, those systems that have run unchanged for years, and which no-one dares touch may be left to run in peace, although eventually 'something will have to be done'! Finally, those systems which are better suited to the old platform should also be left alone. The engineering adage 'if it ain't broke, don't fix it' applies here. Given that most of the world's commercial OLTP systems run on IBM mainframes, using CICS or IMS, it may well be that such systems will be the last to migrate. Indeed, there is a current school of thought that what is left in the old environment should be repackaged as a server, even as a collection of 'objects'. Almost certainly it provides a set of well-defined functions – it only remains, perhaps, to make those functions available via DCE, for example, to bring them into line with the new environment. We have christened this process left-sizing, to go along with right-sizing and down-sizing: it denotes the management of what's left after down-sizing, right-sizing and plain old migration have taken place.

There needs to be a good reason for migrating *any* systems to the new platform: doing it just because it is fashionable is a mistake. One motivator to replace old systems which is gaining momentum is the concept of 're-engineering' business processes. What this entails is a complete rethink of the way that businesses handle their day-to-day transactions in the light of business pressures and of the possibilities offered by technology. The classic example of this is in insurance, where companies have reduced the time taken to issue a new policy from weeks to hours. In this case, it is done by handling the various checks and reviews in parallel, rather than sequentially, something which demands that paper be replaced by electronic images. Clearly if a business process is to be re-engineered, it is very likely that the supporting system will need to be redesigned as well, and this is a good moment to consider migration to client/server design.

The last option is simply to re-write the existing application for the new platform. This is probably sensible if the old platform is expensive to operate or if there is only a small number of systems running on it. The savings from reducing the number of operational platforms are always considerable. Consider using a specialist software house for this – there are some who will offer a high-quality, fixed-price service.

Coexistence

Given that client/server systems will be running alongside older systems for some little while, it clearly makes sense to provide suitable levels of integration between them (Figure 5.2). We have already discussed one important mechanism, namely the copying of data from the production systems to the server.

At some point, it may be necessary to copy data in the other direction, as, for example, when new systems are developed on the server,

Figure 5.2
Coexistence.

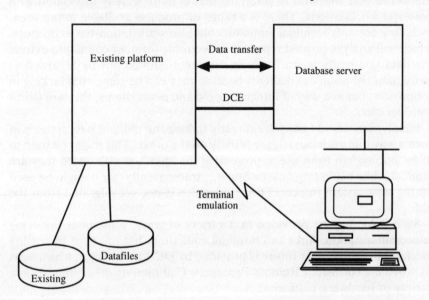

Figure 5.3
Nirvana.

which gather data needed by the production systems. This movement of data between systems may become a very important feature of the computer room, and sophisticated mechanisms to manage it either acquired or developed.

Equally, it may be necessary for some users to have access to both the 'data warehouse' and the old production system. This is usually best done by installing a terminal emulator on the workstation. This provides a very simple link to both environments, which can be further improved by using workstation software 'front-end' which drives the emulator, while providing to the user the kind of interface that is more usually associated with powerful workstations. There is a range of products available in this area, including not only terminal emulators but also workstation-based products which will analyze printed reports (in electronic form, of course) to extract the data you really want. Such arrangements should not be regarded as more than temporary expedients because they can be somewhat lacking in robustness, but as a way of integrating old and new systems, they are worth consideration.

Finally, one should consider directly linking the old and new systems in such a way that each can trigger activity on the other. This might be used to 'hide' one system from users, presenting the interface with which they are familiar while exploiting new technology transparently. Or it might be used on the new system to access function which is not yet migrated from the old.

Such links may be provided in a variety of ways, sometimes involving telecommunications links and terminal emulation, but the most promising mechanism for the near future is provided by DCE technology, which aims to provide a consistent Remote Procedure Call (among other things) on a variety of hardware platforms.

There is little excuse for not starting Phase 1. It need not be an expensive project, and it may provide greater business benefits than anyone expected (Figure 5.3). Subsequent phases can be taken on as seems most suitable, and, of course, they need not be done in the order described. What it should demonstrate is that users are quite capable of handling powerful tools, and the complexities of their data, and that new function really can be delivered fast by such users, in cooperation with IT specialists. As time goes by, not only will the capabilities of these tools increase but also the system management issues will be understood and tackled by appropriate tools, allowing later phases to be undertaken with confidence.

Client/server systems and their impact on people

The advent of powerful workstations and LANs has turned the world of computing on its head. While this is probably good news in the long term, it does mean that the established IT community is feeling under threat. For many years the PC has been written off as a toy, not worthy the attention of serious computer people.

Their attitude is, in psychological terms, all too understandable! And they were given plenty of support for their assertion by the early implementation of PCs on desks, where it seemed that all the lessons of computing had to be relearned: the lessons largely being that systems management is still crucial to a successful installation.

It is now plain for all to see, however, that these PCs have developed into powerful workstations and servers, and that they can deliver astonishing benefits to organizations. This is bad news for the high priests of IT, many of whose existing skills are rendered obsolete, and whose power-base (the large IT budget) is under threat from disillusioned senior management.

Many organizations have developed very substantial DP departments, staffed with analysts, COBOL programmers, database administrators, systems analysts and other creations of the DP world. In a separate organization, they very often have a PC department, too, skilled in MS-DOS, Windows, spreadsheet, word processing and other useful packages. Needless to say, the two departments rarely meet, and view each other with mutual suspicion (Table 5.1).

Ready to heap coals on the fire are a new generation of experienced users who have become very frustrated by the IT department (which appears to them to be delivering too little too late for too much). In many cases, they have declared UDI to a greater or lesser extent, and bought computers of their own, masquerading in their budgets as filing systems or oscilloscopes.

Into this maelstrom steps the unwary designer of client/server systems, whose solutions to business problems require that creative teams of users,

Table 5.1

	Central IT dept	PC dept
Average age	42	21
Preferred languages	COBOL, Assembler	C, C++, Visual Basic
Preferred interface	Command level	WIMP
Preferred coding schema	EBCDIC	ASCII
Preferred comms basis	Synchronous	Asynchronous
Preferred supplier	IBM	Microsoft
View of computing	Hard work	Fun
Spiritual home	Detroit	San Francisco
Development timescale	3 years	20 minutes
Problem resolution	Back out	Reboot
Systems management . . .	is crucial	gets in the way

IT professionals and workstation specialists work enthusiastically together! This human side of computer systems must not be ignored by management wanting to get the best from its staff.

One radical solution to this set of problems is to hand it over to someone else – that is, to 'outsource' the entire computer operation. The contract usually involves fixing the costs of computing for the next five years and moving the IT personnel to work for the out-sourcing company. In some cases, it also involves contracting the outsourcing company to rewrite existing systems based on 'open' hardware and software platforms, with the objective of handing back the IT operation to the company in a state where it is significantly cheaper to run.

The attractions of such a solution are obvious – senior management has at least fixed its operating costs for a period, and has shed a large and difficult personnel problem. It remains to be seen whether those contracts will be viewed as a sensible step with hindsight, but if the analogy of computing with electricity generation has any merit, it does at least raise the question about whether companies should plan to run their own IT departments or whether they should outsource: precious few companies generate their own electricity. On the other hand, IT systems are closely wedded to core business activities, and its delegation to a third party is not to be undertaken lightly.

This resolves the human problems in a somewhat brutal fashion, by off-loading them onto someone else. It also brings the danger of losing key IT personnel altogether, those who not only understand IT but also how the systems support the particular business.

The ultimate solution to the human issues lies in concepts like motivation, retraining and leadership. There is no doubt that most IT departments have too many skills of the wrong sort and not enough of the new. This problem needs to be squarely faced. Some existing skills will continue to be in demand, and systems management embraces many of them. Database design and data integrity will clearly become a focal point for the

IT department. The data network will be a crucial part of the new IT infrastructure.

New skills will be needed – largely to do with the exploitation of workstations. Some of these can be acquired by existing staff, given the right training and motivation. Others may need to be recruited.

Perhaps the most difficult thing to change in existing IT staff will be their expectations: they currently have an idea of how long certain things take, like developing new function for users. That needs to be reduced by an order of magnitude. They also tend to think in terms of 'applications', by which is meant the automation of a large section of the business, such as Accounts Receivable. They need to start thinking in terms of discrete pieces of user function (the word 'objects' could be used here).

At the end of the day, however, it is very likely that IT departments will need to be slimmed down. They have, in the case of many companies, become a huge drain on resources, which can be ill-afforded during recessionary times. It is ironic that this new wave of computer capability should bring with it a decline in IT staffs.

The final group of people to be considered in all of this are the users. However frustrated they may feel about their existing IT systems, they have to a large extent been spoon-fed by it. In future, they will be given a set of tools on a workstation and told to get on with it! This will need a change in attitude from them as well.

They will certainly need to become more involved in the data-processing environment, meaning that they will need to understand their data thoroughly, know how to manipulate the tools available to them, and be ready to learn new tools. The body of people known as 'knowledge workers' will increasingly depend on computer tools for their livelihood.

If there is any truth in the assertion that client/server systems can deliver easy access to data, then it also becomes inescapably true that any layer of management whose job is primarily to collate data from below them in the hierarchy and relay it higher up the chain is under threat of redundancy. That acquisition of data will be handled by computer systems. The truth of this can be seen in the wave of redundancies that has occurred in the 1992/3 recession: companies have been stripping out layers of management altogether, moving to flatter organizations. This was a white-collar recession more than any other.

Summary

- Migration should start with those systems which can most benefit from client/server computing – the data warehouse may be a good concept to consider.
- Whole applications need not be migrated – perhaps just the reporting phases.

- There will be a long period of coexistence between the existing systems and the new. This can be achieved at the terminal level, the application level and the data level.
- Change is usually difficult for people. This new way of computing will impose personal stress on existing IT departments, which should be handled with understanding.

6 Costs

One of the benefits rightly claimed for client/server computing is that it allows companies to exploit the low price/performance ratios available today on workstations and on 'open' servers. Unfortunately, this is not to say that client/server computing is cheap or easy to cost-justify. We shall discuss this dilemma in what follows.

The first point to make is that hardware costs are declining in the mainframe world as well as in the 'open' one. There is competition, even in proprietary systems, and usually a healthy second-hand market. As a result, hardware costs are no longer the major component of an IT budget. Second, one is rarely dealing these days with a company that has no computing at all – more likely, there already exists a computer system and it is very likely to comprise a mainframe and some 'dumb' terminals. Consequently, one is often comparing the *marginal* cost of installing an enhancement to an existing system with the *absolute* cost of installing a client/server system. This leads to comparisons between dumb terminals and PC-based workstations, in which the latter will appear to be five times as expensive to a financial controller. Equally, a company may view unfavourably the need to install a costly LAN infrastructure instead of using the existing wiring. Third, one is suggesting a need for new skills, purchased probably from outside the company as opposed to exploiting existing ones, available within. Finally, one is probably not able to make any savings in the existing infrastructure, which will have to run on for many years. On the contrary, some upgrades to the existing system may well be needed to provide data connectivity to the new.

In short, the introduction of client/server technology is likely to be a significant additional cost. The only way to justify such a cost is by demonstrating that the new system can be built and delivered much more quickly with client/server techniques than with traditional methods. As long as there is a sound business case behind the new application, the increased cost may be justified.

There are other areas of cost which we should pursue. It is perceived that large mainframe systems need expensive support staff such as systems programmers. What they do not need are staff to support the powerful workstations and departmental servers which come as part of the client/ server way of life. Some migrations have run into trouble precisely because the support requirements have been underestimated, and either not provided in time or not funded properly.

There are some costs which increase directly with growth in client/server systems: examples are hardware, software, and support staff. The costs do not increase linearly, but they do increase. They are not linear because, for example, the costs of a hundred workstations is likely to be less than ten times the cost of ten workstations. Equally, software licences get cheaper as the quantity increases.

Some costs increase in a less predictable way: these are associated with overall system management. For example, software distribution on ten workstations can be handled as a tiresome manual task for an initial project: it must be properly handled, and probably automated, by the time a hundred workstations is reached. The same thinking applies to network management, problem management, asset management, security management: in all these cases there comes a point where an informal system which may be adequate for a small number of users breaks down and *must* be replaced with a properly controlled process. This will inevitably involve spending money, but just how much money is particularly difficult to assess.

The difficulty is compounded by the fact that new management tools are appearing on a regular basis and their capability is improving, as is their quality. Furthermore, the increasing competition is keeping prices in check. Consequently a management task such as remote software management may seem difficult and costly today, but will probably be much simplified in twelve months' time.

Excessive heterogeneity should be avoided: that is, limit the number of suppliers involved in the client/server environment. One of the pleasures of open client/server systems is that one has an array of vendors to choose from for almost every component of the system. Tasting these pleasures must be tempered with common sense: a system built from components from ten different vendors is more likely to develop problems, and cost more to manage, than one from three vendors.

It must also be admitted that there are likely to be some hidden costs associated with installing powerful workstations around the company. Such tasks as replacing toner cartridges in printers, adding paper, problem determination, software upgrading, filing manuals can become user tasks if no-one has thought of providing for them. These can be time consuming and irksome, and difficult to quantify.

We have discussed the cost of installing a LAN, which can be considerable. We must also consider any wide area networks. The design of the system can have a significant effect on network loading and this can have repercussions on the expense of the network. As discussed in Chapter 4, sending SQL requests and data replies over the network can involve much more network traffic than a network request for an application to perform data manipulation on a local database. Also, two-phase commit for systems that generate a lot of updates over a network will add extra loading.

Some say that a client/server system always imposes a high load on the network, but this is far from a general rule. A client/server system certainly generates a different pattern of network traffic, and may benefit from higher bandwidth.

Cost avoidance

It will probably be tempting to trim the hardware cost by reducing the specification of the client workstations: do we really need 486 processors? Couldn't we get away with 386 machines? These are valid questions, and much money has been wasted on purchasing the latest technology irrespective of the requirement. However, one must not lose sight of the probability that requirements for the client will grow over time, with new releases of software and new facilities being offered. A short-term saving may turn into a long-term loss.

Another likely avenue for saving costs is to re-use existing equipment for a new task, with the obvious example being the use of a mainframe as a database server. This is a perfectly valid exercise, and should be explored. It is, however, important to include *all* the costs in such an exercise: it is not unknown for the maintenance costs alone to exceed the overall costs of new technology.

A tempting mechanism which exploits the mainframe, existing software and terminal wiring and thus reduces cost is that of terminal emulation, which was discussed earlier. This is a perfectly valid mechanism, and used to good effect in many places, but it is unlikely to be a long-term solution, rather a way of getting started easily. This being so, the costs (of terminal emulator cards, for instance) should be written off over a fairly short period. Again, a short-term saving may result in a long-term loss.

Politics

A layer of complication in costing a migration to client/server systems is provided by the budgeting and planning arrangements in place in many large companies. They can also provide useful battlegrounds on which the existing IT organization can fight its rearguard actions! The way in which existing services are costed on the central system is very often a mystery to the users, and in truth, a matter more of politics than real cost. As a result, when a new initiative threatens to replace an existing service, the cost of that service can miraculously be reduced by the central IT department, undermining the whole project. By contrast, a user department which is enthusiastic to try out the benefits of client/server systems can take the workstation and LAN costs onto its own budget as a legitimate local expenditure, leaving only the central server to be included in the project.

Where, then, does all this jiggery-pokery leave us? It usually means that a move to client/server is only likely to happen if a genuine opportunity exists to improve the operation of some part of the company by its use. This means finding a project that has an undeniable benefit, such as fraud detection, well-targeted marketing, or improved customer service and which can best be provided in client/server style. It is operational improvements to the company rather than cost savings which are most likely to lead to a successful move to client/server systems.

It also means that a system constructed of 'dumb' terminals and a central mainframe or mini may be the right solution to a given company's requirements. Client/server systems provide immense power to competent users, and can help transform the whole 'modus operandi' of a company. If what is required is a simple accounting system, however, it may be that a well-tried package running on a central system supplied and supported by a single vendor is the optimal choice.

Summary

- Client/server computing is different from centralized computing, and costs are not directly comparable.
- Installing the first client/server system or migrating one's entire IT infrastructure to client/server operation is almost certainly going to cost money, at least in the short term.
- Some of the costs are obvious, some are not. There are long-term as well as short-term costs to be considered. Costs can be manipulated by departments for their own political ends.
- Significant benefits to the company should be clearly visible before embarking in any major way on this course. These are likely to come from faster reaction to market forces, better utilization of existing data and better customer service.
- In the long term, savings may also accrue from a significant reduction in the development effort needed for new applications.

7 Migration case study

Introduction

The Air Products – Europe Group is an industrial gases and chemicals manufacturing company employing about 3000 staff and operates in 13 European countries. The European headquarters is located in Hersham, Surrey. The company has an IT department of about 130, 60 of whom are developers in the area of commercial business systems. There is a small number of data centre support staff in Germany, France and Belgium.

The computer architecture – before

The architecture comprised a mainframe located in the USA linked via high-speed fiber-optic circuits to a distributed network of HP3000s located at the European headquarters and in France, Belgium and Germany. Two additional systems are installed at the headquarters to provide development and data communication 'hub' facilities. This infrastructure also supports the provision of electronic mail (Figure 7.1).

Criteria for change

Since 1979 the company has consistently reviewed its information system requirements as part of its business-planning process. A formal information systems strategic plan is produced linking identified applications development to business goals and strategy. As part of this process an information technology plan is produced specifying technology and infrastructure requirements. In January 1992, the information systems planning process identified a number of changes that were occurring both within the company and the external marketplace. These were:

1. A number of small, standalone PC-based applications had been installed, quickly, cheaply and effectively.

Figure 7.1
Legacy system.

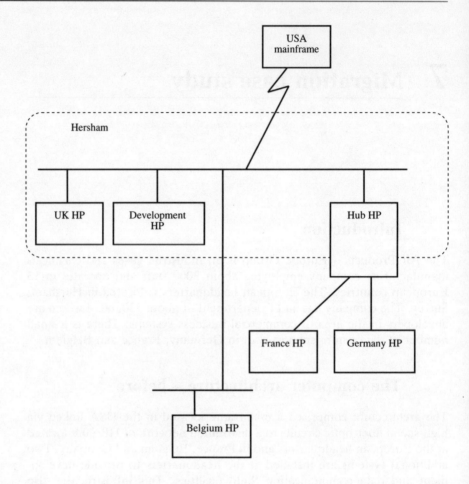

2.   Staff were becoming familiar with MS-Windows and its GUI-style of interface. The number of PCs in use was growing rapidly (it doubled from 700 within the three years from 1990).
3.   There was a clear move in the industry towards open systems.
4.   Network costs were declining and capabilities increasing.
5.   A need for new data types such as voice and image was identified.

The main criteria for the new architecture were established as:

- *Window on the world*. Access from any PC to any corporate data through appropriate applications.
- *Corporate data access architecture*. From a technical viewpoint, a consistent means by which applications could access all corporate data, including legacy data (hierarchical and network databases), current

general-purpose data (relational databases), specialized data (e.g. CAD/CAM, external data sources) and future types of information (image, voice, 'objects').

- *Integrated data management*. Ability to manage and access data distributed across different platforms as an integrated whole.
- *Packaged software availability*. Access to a range of third-party software that does not compromise data management objectives.

Key characteristics of the strategic database included:

- *Server-based integrity*. To protect the data from the increasingly wide range of PC-based applications that may access corporate databases. This was also seen as a key element of re-usability to deliver development productivity gains.
- *Efficient, scalable server platform*. The relational database had to be fully supported, with full connectivity, across a range of hardware platforms, from PC servers supporting one to ten users in a cost-effective way to larger servers capable of supporting up to 100–200 concurrent users.
- *Resilience for on-line systems*. Sufficient resilience and availability features were required to support mission-critical applications.
- *Access to new forms of data*. We needed a statement of direction on support for new forms of information such as voice and image. Connectivity of the database product was, of course, a key requirement. LANs were beginning to develop and standards for connectivity products were already in place. A specific requirement was connectivity with Air Products parent company Air Products and Chemicals Inc. in Pennsylvania, to provide global capabilities.
- *PC Windows clients*. The worldwide network standard is MS LAN Manager running over NetBEUI and TCP/IP.
- *Choice of end-user and development tools*. Business application requirements range from mainstream GUI development to specialized areas (e.g. geographical systems, linear programming, handheld applications) and newer technologies (e.g. multimedia). It was important that development tools existed to support these requirements on our chosen database platform.
- *MPE COBOL applications*. As well as access to legacy data from PC applications a requirement existed for access to relational data from our existing applications. This was viewed as a long transition phase.
- *Gateways to other ISV databases*. We planned to standardize where possible on a single relational database. However niche applications already existed which held data in other forms (CAD/CAM, expert systems) and we expected this to continue. We therefore required access via gateway products to these data stores.

Strategy

A strategy was defined to pursue a three-pronged approach:

- Database infrastructure
- Application development tools
- Systems development methodology

The database infrastructure was seen as the foundation of the architecture and evaluation of appropriate database products began in May 1992. When this evaluation was well advanced we began looking at development tools which matched the database product we expected to select. Experience in the use of a PC-based GUI development tool was gained before consideration was given to a system development methodology.

Database evaluation

Air Products began working with database vendors in May 1992 utilizing very comprehensive evaluation criteria. Examples of some of the key criteria are referenced as follows:

- Performance
- Support
- Pricing
- Long- and short-term costs
- Company viability
- Relationship
- Fit with worldwide corporate architecture
- Availability of third-party packages for potential future requirements and specific known needs.

Sources of data for the evaluation were vendor presentations, industry reports and meetings with and visits to other customer sites. In August, as a result of our preliminary evaluation, Sybase SQL server was installed for a six-week trial period. The final decision on the database had not yet been taken and this period was invaluable in highlighting technical issues and gaining experience in the new environment.

After the successful completion of the trial we had a much better idea of the technical requirements and were able to specify and cost what was needed. There was then a period of negotiation before a contract was finally signed with Sybase in February 1993.

Implementation

Microsoft SQL Server had been in place in Air Products for some time. From April 1993 application development commenced with the objective of migrating to Sybase SQL server. Initially, two HP9000 servers were installed to run Sybase SQL Server: a development server with 32MB of memory and a 3GB disk and a 64MB production server with 5GB of disk storage. Later a third server was installed in Belgium.

Application development against Sybase SQL server began in August 1993 and all the development databases were migrated from Microsoft SQL Server to Sybase by the end of August. Key accomplishments were:

- First applications released in pilot form – May 1993
- Two HP9000 UNIX servers and Sybase SQL Server installed – June 1993
- Application development against Sybase SQL server commenced – August 1993
- Databases migrated from OS/2 to UNIX – August 1993
- Evaluation of development methodologies commenced – June 1993
- Pilot group of programmer/analysts undertake development methodology training – July 1993

Application development tools

Evaluation of application development tools began after the database evaluation was well under way and a clearer picture was emerging of the eventual architecture. Development tools were evaluated in September and October 1992. An essential requirement here was the need for synergy with our parent company who had already established a GUI development tool but not a 'corporate' relational database. We perceived that common development tools would allow integration of applications and joint applications development. Powersoft's PowerBuilder was eventually chosen and pilot development began late in 1992 with the first small-scale applications released in May 1993 running against Microsoft SQL Server as we had not yet installed Sybase SQL Server.

Systems development methodology

The third strand of the strategy, systems development methodology, began in earnest in mid-1993. A development team was trained in July 1993 and a pilot of the methodology is being used on a single project. The pilot is to be reviewed later in 1994 when a decision will be made on whether to adopt the methodology.

The main issue that has emerged during this period of quite radical change has been that of training. We invested in external training in our adopted GUI development tool and developed internal courses in SQL. The SQL training requirement, however, proved to be greater than we envisaged. Developers do need to write a great deal of SQL during application development particularly if, as in our case, database access is handled through stored procedures rather than embedded SQL, which is largely generated by the development tool. In addition to knowledge of the syntax of the language, developers must understand performance, transaction management and multi-user issues. A third area of training is interface design, and here our approach has been to identify and communicate best practices. The quality of our application interfaces varies widely. Some people appear to have an innate ability in this area, but certainly a mainframe background is not a great help!

The computer architecture – after

Three HP9000/UNIX servers run Sybase SQL Server. SQL Server is accessed either from MS Windows PCs or from a COBOL application running on an HP3000 which accesses SQL Server via a custom-built gateway. PCs can access SQL Server from in-house developed Power-Builder applications but it can also use *ad hoc* query packages such as Microsoft Access and Pioneer's Q+E. Data is regularly copied from legacy systems into SQL Server databases (Figure 7.2).

This may be represented in LEGHAWK notation thus:

System $=$ $(SYS_{hp3000}$ I $SYS_{pc})$ $>\sim Ce\sim <([D_{sydev}]_{unix}|[D_{syuk}]_{unix}|$
$[Dsybel]_{unix}$

$SYS_{pc} = [P\text{-Apbwin} | \ldots\ldots\ldots\ldots]_{pc}$

$SYS_{hp3000} = [PA_{cobol} \sim R_{tigwy}]$

$P\text{-A}_{pbwin} = \{nSess=ML; \ PresInt=MSWin; \ PresIPCProt=CutPaste,$
     $DDE \ MsgType=Sync; \ Lang=PowerBuilder\}$

$Ce = \{Mech=Socket, Cable=Ethernet, Proto=TCP\}$

$D_{sydev} = \{Prod='SQL \ Server'; \ Ver='4.92'; \ Vendor='SYBASE';$
     $memory=32M;disk=1G\}$

$D_{sy} = \{Prod='SQL \ Server'; \ Ver='4.92'; \ Vendor='SYBASE'; \ memory$
     $=64M;disk=2G\}$

$[\ ]_{unix} = \{Model=HP3000; OpSys='UNIX'.\}$

Summary

There is an almost infinite number of combinations of products that can be brought together as a client/server architecture. This gives the customers the flexibility to develop solutions to their own unique business problems. The downside of flexibility, however, is increasing complexity. The architecture that suits the operations of any sizeable corporation is likely to be unique to that corporation, and although the experience of similar organizations will be useful you certainly cannot, to date, buy client/server solutions off the shelf.

The major technical issue that we faced during the evaluation and implementation phases was connectivity. This included legacy data on mainframe and mini platforms and the connection of 'legacy' applications

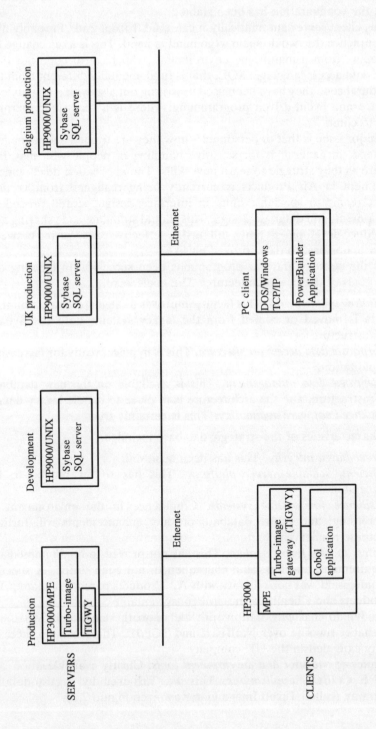

Figure 7.2
Client/server design.

to relational databases. The solution was a custom-built gateway. Once in place, the configuration has been stable.

Does client/server automatically mean a GUI front-end? Probably not, but in practice the two do seem to go hand in hand. This is a sea change for developers from a mainframe environment, who have to cope not only with a data access language, SQL, that is fundamentally different from the procedural code they have been used to writing but also with a new style of interface and event-driven programming. There is a very steep learning curve to climb.

A major issue is that of personnel – how they are trained and managed. The need, in general, is for sensitive handling of people who may feel insecure as they struggle to learn new skills. The application development department in Air Products is currently being realigned from vertical project teams to specialist units in interface design, stored procedure development, and database design. This should stimulate code sharing and thus reduce development times still further: effective code sharing between project teams has, to date, proved elusive.

Has the strategy and our programmes been successful in meeting the initial goals of the new architecture? The goals were:

- *Window on the world*. This facility improves as an increasing amount of data is moved or copied from the legacy systems onto the Sybase infrastructure.
- *Corporate data access architecture*. This is in place, ready for increasing exploitation.
- *Integrated data management*. This is available on the new database infrastructure, and the architecture is in place to handle legacy data.
- *Packaged software availability*. This is certainly true.

Key characteristics of the strategic database included:

- *Server-based integrity*. This has been achieved.
- *Efficient, scalable server platform*. This has so far proved to be successful.
- *Resilience for on-line systems*. Confidence in the environment is increasing, and future database product enhancements will further increase resilience.
- *Access to new forms of data*. This has not proved to be an immediate requirement, and has, as a consequence, not been tested. A specific requirement was connectivity with Air Products parent company, Air Products and Chemicals Inc. in Pennsylvania.
- *PC Windows clients*. The worldwide network standard is MS LAN Manager running over NetBEUI and TCP/IP. This has been success-fully extended to the UK company.
- *Choice of end-user and development tools*. Clearly available.
- *MPE COBOL applications*. This was achieved by a custom-built gateway (called Turbo Image Gateway – see Figure 7.2).

- *Gateways to other ISV databases.* Omni SQL is currently providing access to an Oracle database used in a niche application.

In summary, the architectural goals have been achieved, the only doubts being in respect of 'mission-critical' levels of reliability and access to new data types.

Air Products has installed two new applications using the new architecture, the first being a system to provide a standard purchase requisition capability. This was successfully implemented, and has eliminated the paperwork associated with the previous process. It has proved to be an excellent means for development personnel to gain experience of radically new technology with 'low-risk' business impact.

Experience gained from this development has enabled us to move with confidence to the second application, which provides a centralized 'customer care' capability. This is part of a re-engineered process for handling customer enquiries. Success with this application has been achieved through the exploitation of powerful workstations integrated with relational databases and 'client/server' design being used to provide the requirements of a radically re-engineered process.

8 Case study – the Prefix architecture

In 1986, Synergo Technology Ltd took the business decision to build a settlement system to sell to brokers dealing in shares. Some founding members of the company had used Tandem's server requester mechanisms (that is the early 1980s way of saying client/server), and were impressed with the way it split the screen handling from the application servers. The technical team (two of us) built on this and began the design of an architecture that used a graphical user interface on a PC and application servers on a mini. The design had to consider:

- This is a classic OLTP type of application
  - Many users using the same applications
  - Interactions are short-lived
  - Large database
- The user interface would be standard across all applications to ease training and cut down on user errors. Also there was real concern that when developers took control of screen interfaces, the result was too often a mess. Each developer would have different ways of dealing with input (validating a field when it is filled, and/or on CR, and/or on TAB), different uses of colour and function keys, different ways of dealing with validation errors, and handling validation of interrelated fields. Screens become so individualistic that there could be a severe learning curve for a user being introduced to a new application. The new architecture should remove the responsibility of the screen behaviour from the application developer.
- The user interface would do domain checking. Thus the application servers need not validate the format of the incoming data.
- It should be possible to alter screens without modifying the server. Thus if some customers wanted fields in a different order, or with different prompts, then the server would remain the same.
- The user interface should allow the user to type ahead, i.e. the interface should allow the user to enter a new request while the previous request is still being processed.

- The host part of the architecture must be easily ported to other platforms. The initial development was to be on VAX/VMS, but the settlement system must be able to be sold to customers with other operating systems.
- The servers must be written in COBOL (to take advantage of Synergo's skills).

There were other server requirements that emerged from our collective experience of other computer systems that we had worked on:

- We wanted to use a RDBMS
- We must minimize the parsing overhead for embedded SQL (ESQL)
- Data records were not to be locked for long periods
- Context–free programs were easier to write and to maintain
- Ease of maintenance is of paramount importance
- Ideally, the server code should be concerned only with business logic

Designing Prefix

Initially, we looked at the type of interactions that a user has with an OLTP system, and came up with

- Input of new data
- Amending old data
- Deleting data
- Enquiring on data

We found that a user interacts with an OLTP application in only a few well-defined ways, which we mapped to a three-letter 'objective' for each client/server interaction

Entering an application	APF
Asking for a record	KEY
Validating a field	FVA
Updating a record	TUP
Abandoning a transaction	ABN

We designed both the user interface and the server logic around these concepts. When a user asks for a record when using the amend function of an application, a message with the KEY objective and the A function would be sent to the server, along with the data in the key fields, and the data would be returned.

In order to decouple the user interface from the server we introduced the concept of numbering the fields. Each screen field had two numbers – the positional number, which described its position on the screen, and the actual number, by which it was known to the server. All messages between the client and server hold the data by actual number. The client process must map between the positional number and the actual number. This way, the screen can be rearranged without affecting the server.

The user interface

In 1986 we had the choice between two emerging GUI products for PCs – Gem and Windows. On balance, Gem looked and behaved better than Windows 1. But Gem had no developer's kit, so it had to be Windows.

We designed a simple uncluttered interface, with a single field per line. Each line consists of a prompt and input area, and a message area for displaying error messages or enrichments. The use of colour and fonts was used sparingly to show important attributes of fields, such as whether a field is mandatory, non-input, in error, or not yet validated. The cursor, by default, always moves down the screen, which scrolls if necessary.

The user interface is a single program that reads in screen parameters from files on the PC. These files describe the fields, their attributes and how this application links to others. These parameter files define the field types, local lookup lists, and how a field can link to a server to list the available values from the database.

As a number of application sessions can be running simultaneously, we developed a method of mapping fields from one application to and from another. This means that a user can press a Link key when on a Customer field in a Bargain application, and another copy of the user interface will load up with the Customer Enquiry application displaying the details of that customer, using the mapping information.

Recently we have taken these ideas further, and have made our user interface DDE aware. Then we built Visual Basic custom controls, so that we can build Visual Basic applications from a mix and match of fields from different Prefix applications. This moves away from the strict and simple screen design of the original user interface, but allows our customers to effectively design their own screens around the functionality of the existing applications. Existing applications are now the screen building blocks for more complex business functions.

Server design

In traditional architectures, when a record is accessed for update it stays locked against other users until that process does the update. This means that there has to be a data area in the server for each client to hold the lock information. Therefore the server cannot be context-free, and code is necessary to keep track of which client processes are at which stage of the transaction cycle. Also, all messages from a client would have to be passed to the same copy of the server. If other servers were to access that record, they would effectively hang until the record is freed. So one slow user could freeze out other users.

We decided early on that we were going to use soft-locking, whereby a user session can reserve data records, with a time-out. We implemented this by using extra dedicated data fields on each record on every table, and defining strict rules on the use of these fields. These are used to hold, as data in the database, information about locks. The advantages are these:

- The server no longer needs a data area per client
- Any copy of the server can handle client requests, helping load balancing
- No servers hang on record locks – they can report back to the user that the data is reserved
- Communications failure doesn't leave records locked, as the locks time out.

We built a standard COBOL template, which handles the program control flow and calls a number of sub-units to deal with common functionality – e.g. error message handling, mapping from message structures to COBOL data areas, checking and setting soft-locks. The template is arranged in such a way that section and variable names are standardized. The programmer adds in the business code in the relevant area. For example, there is a section that is called whenever a FVA Amend message is received, and the programmer adds code to validate the fields. A standard layout makes maintenance easier, as all the programmers know where the code should be.

In order to be able to port this business logic to other platforms we built a layer of code in C, called the C shell, which is linked with the COBOL executable, to provide system services. This is again a standard set of APIs to let the COBOL access system services, such as interprocess communications and semaphores. As the COBOL can then be ANSI standard, porting to another platform becomes porting the small set of routines that is the C shell.

Once started, a server would stay active until terminated. A server does a blocked read on a mailbox, reads a message, performs what is required, sends the reply, and then waits for another message. The parsing of the ESQL is only done the first time the statement is processed, so subsequent processing is much faster.

Code generator

In simple applications the fields on the screen correspond to the columns of one table in the database. The mapping from screen to database columns are therefore known, the program flow is determined by the architecture and user interactions, and the code layout is determined by the standards of the template. Therefore we could generate all the COBOL code, including all the copybooks and ESQL, which would run a simple application without host validation at field level.

The time savings for the developers were such that they asked us to provide a cut-down version to produce just the Oracle access modules, given a table definition. Now they use these code fragments to glue together a significant portion of complex applications. The field validations are not generated, as we believe that the language required to fully describe our requirements for validation would not be much simpler than COBOL itself. Simple lookups are trivial to code, calling the generated ESQL. We call our Code Generator a 3½ GL. Given that nearly all 4GLs have user exits (i.e. a place to put your own 3GL code where the 4GL can't describe your requirement), I think ours is more like 3¾ GL.

The code generator has only recently been developed. We know it drastically decreases development time, and are hoping that by reducing the amount of code the programmers actually get to touch, it will reduce errors. Also, it will help us to reduce the number of cases where programmers break our in-house coding standards that have been developed to ease porting to UNIX and to MVS (DB2 has its own limitations, as we found out to our cost). All development is done on our VAX, which is too forgiving of programmer errors which then show up on UNIX.

Architecture design

Communications

PC to host – Asynch

We had to be able to communicate with any type of host machine, and did not want to get heavily involved in how binary numbers were stored on different platforms. Therefore we chose a string representation of all numbers, and used string-to-number and number-to-string conversions, which all platforms should provide. The message packet was made up of a header, with field attributes and data delimited with a special character. This delimiting of data lead to much smaller packet lengths than using fixed lengths for all data areas in the packet.

Initially, we used the concept of a communications controller, which sat on a NetBIOS-based LAN to communicate with the host machine, using RS232 asynchronous messages. We built a communications module that ran as a separate task under Windows, and talked an early version of DDE (Dynamic Data Exchange) with the user interface task. This used NetBIOS NCB calls to communicate with the controller, on a separate PC, which buffered messages and handled all communications with the mini host (Figure 8.1).

Figure 8.1
Original configuration
– rejected.

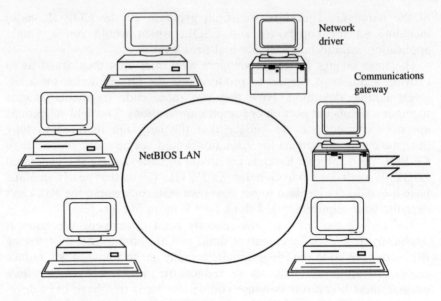

Network
driver

Communications
gateway

NetBIOS LAN

Figure 8.2
Final configuration for
RS232 connections.

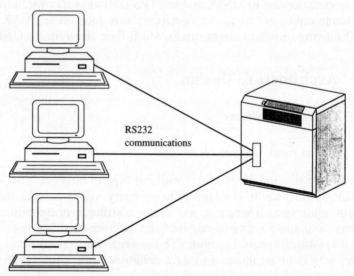

RS232
communications

This solution was soon rejected. It was too expensive and complex – a dedicated controller PC was required, as well as a dedicated PC to drive the Netbios LAN. There was likely to be problems driving more than one asynch port from the one controller PC, and all the PCs needed LAN cards.

We simplified this enormously by using the built-in communications port on each PC and making the receiver program on the host capable of

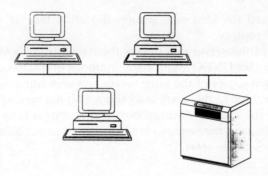

Figure 8.3
TCP/IP configuration.

dealing with many physical ports. Thus no network was required and no extra PCs (Figure 8.2).

PC to host – TCP/IP sockets

The TCP/IP sockets interface presented us with a problem. When we first decided to move down this route there was only one supplier of a sockets library under Windows – and that only worked in Real mode! Over the years, other suppliers have produced more sophisticated socket develop-ment kits for Windows, but each vendor has their own interface. So we had to write a new sockets interface to Windows for each TCP/IP vendor that our customers were using or preferred to use. In early 1993 the Windows Socket API was published, and most vendors are promising to adhere to it. This will mean that our single-sockets interface will work with any vendor's TCP/IP stack provided they are compliant with this specification (Figure 8.3).

Interprocess communication within the host

On the VMS host we built a router that would accept messages from the PC client, decide which server should handle the message, and pass it on to the server's mailbox. The application name and the function (Input, Amend, Delete or Enquire) determine the server.

Under VMS, the design of the router took advantage of ASTs (Asynch-ronous Service Traps) to trap for external events, such as a message arriving over a port or from a mailbox. The router is, therefore, interrupt-driven. At first we thought that the router may become a bottleneck for the system, as all messages must pass through it, so we built in the ability to run multiple routers. This implies some simple controlling mechanism to determine to which router a new connection should be assigned. In practice, the router on the VAX was never a bottleneck, and this facility was never required. However, when we graduated to a TCP/IP sockets interface a few years later on UNIX platforms, some flavours of UNIX restricted the number of open devices (be they files or sockets or pipes), so we reintroduced the idea of a session-allocation task as we had to use multiple TCP routers.

The name of the server determines the name of the VMS mailbox (or FIFO name under UNIX). With these methods of interprocess communication, multiple copies of the same server can be waiting on a read of the same mailbox. One of them will read and act on the message and send the reply back to the router's own mailbox. If one copy is busy, another copy will service the next message, so loads will tend to get balanced between multiple copies of the servers.

Process management

As the number of applications, and hence the number of servers, grew over time we had to develop a mechanism to stop and start tasks automatically as required. We could no longer prestart all the servers, as we would swamp the memory and swap areas, and cause thrashing.

We built a suite of small tasks on the host that recorded who was using which applications and set usage parameters to decide when to stop and start tasks. Commonly used tasks would be set to 'never stop', even if currently unused, as there would soon be the overhead of starting and reparsing the SQL. Various parameters can be set, such as the number of users per copy of the server.

In order to implement this we had to introduce a new objective – the END message, so that we could know when a client process was finished with a server. We now had a server-registration mechanism. When an APF or END message was received by the router it would send them to the server management process, which would adjust the registrations and decide whether to stop or start a process. An APF message would then get passed to the server, which sends its reply to the router, and so the user gets to know that the server is now active (Figure 8.4).

Figure 8.4
Message flow.

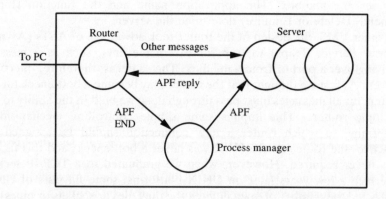

Background servers

In the application suite of programs there were some complex but not urgent tasks that were the result of user interaction. For example, in our settlements system, when a bargain was entered the accounts had to be updated. It had to be done by the end of the day, but could take some seconds for each transaction. Rather than have the user wait for this update after entering a bargain, the server would update its primary tables, put an entry on a request table, set the accounts semaphore, and then reply to the client.

The accounts process waits on the semaphore. When it gets woken, it unsets the semaphore, processes all the entries it can find in its request table, and then waits on its semaphore again. All background servers are designed to drain their request table before waiting on a semaphore, so they will process all outstanding requests, even after the system has been closed down, and no sempahores are set. Some users prevent the background servers from starting up until there is a quiet part of the day, when they can catch up without affecting performance. The process management tasks start background servers if a semaphore has remained unserviced and stops background tasks if they haven't used CPU for a while.

Generalized database selection and dynamic SQL

For business reasons we decided at an early stage to use Oracle RDBMS. Oracle, and possibly other RDBMSs, have an annoying quirk. If you make a request like

```
SELECT * FROM TABLE1 WHERE COL1 LIKE '&1'
```

where &1 is a passed parameter, this will select all rows where COL1 matches the criterion. If you want all rows, then

```
SELECT * FROM TABLE1 WHERE COL1 LIKE '%'
```

will *not* work, as this excludes those rows where COL1 is empty.

```
SELECT * FROM TABLE1 WHERE COL1 LIKE '%' OR COL1 IS NULL
```

will work, but the addition of the NULL means that indexes will not be used, so performance will be appalling. It has to be written as

SELECT * FROM TABLE1

This implies that if multiple selection criteria on fields that can be left empty (i.e. don't care about this value) are offered to users, the selection statement has to be built at run-time. Part of the design of the user interface allows the users to enter selection criteria for the transactions on which they wish to work, and they get a list of matching records. These lists, therefore, require dynamic SQL, which in COBOL stretches the language and the programmer.

To overcome this, we supplied a utility that, when given a select statement and the mapping between actual field numbers and database columns, will generate code that will perform the dynamic SQL according to which incoming fields have data in them. This is written in C. As it is a separate server, we had to have a new function L for List, so the router could send the request to this new server rather than the standard application server.

Security

Access to the host operating system

In order to establish an RS232 asynchronous connection with Prefix, the communications module on the PC invisibly follows a script, which logs on to the system, starts a program that passes control of the line to the host router, and the message passing can begin. This requires therefore a normal user name and password. The TCP/IP connection is via sockets, and the message passing can begin as soon as a socket connection has been established.

Access to Prefix

The first application that runs on the client accepts a user name and password. The server checks against a database to see if the user is allowed to access the system. The checks are against time of access, password expiry, PC restrictions, etc. Only after the logon server has accepted right of access does the client process allow the user to choose other applications.

The application selection process also involves messages to a server to check if that user is allowed access to the application and function. We provide a set of security servers that allow an administrator to set up user groups and application groups and access links between them. One of Synergo's customers has chosen to replace this with their own security server.

Different environments

Prefix offers the users different systems for Testing, Training, Live, etc. Access to each environment is controlled by a socket number over TCP/IP networks or by user name over RS232 communications. The socket number and machine name attaches to a system that is running within an account whose environment variables (or VMS logicals) determine the Oracle database that is being used and the server directory. On the PC the user can have a different set of screen parameter files for each environment. Thus with one PC and one host it is possible to attach to multiple environments.

Performance

Prefix, as an architecture, can support a much larger number of users on a host machine than traditional systems – a factor of 5 to 10 is often quoted. No host I/O is required to paint screens and servers need not validate the format of the data. Interaction with the host is on a message basis, sent only when particular host work is required. Performance problems are usually traceable to poor use of SQL, not enough care in the creation of indices, and bad coding practices in the servers. This would be true under any architecture.

When large numbers of servers are active, normal computer problems of memory and swap space exhaustion affect performance badly. The more memory that can be allocated to Oracle, and be available for servers, the better the system performs. If servers have to be stopped and started often to handle memory contention, then the initialization overheads will affect performance.

In order to measure performance, we built a simulator. Normal use of the system is captured in log files on the PC and replayed through the PC at speed. This is most often used to determine how many copies of a server are required to prevent swamping the system at high usage rates. The simulator can be run at speeds of up to about five messages per second, which is about twenty-five times the speed of a fast user.

External services

As a supplier of software to brokers we have had to provide links to various external suppliers of price data. As these are usually X.25 services, and all hosts have different X.25 mechanisms, we built a communications server on a hefty PC running OS/2, which understands the different protocols of the external services. This converts them to a standard format that is passed via the PC-to-host mechanism (TCP/IP sockets for VAX and UNIX, and APPC for MVS machines). A special router server on the host

Figure 8.5
Communicating with
other services.

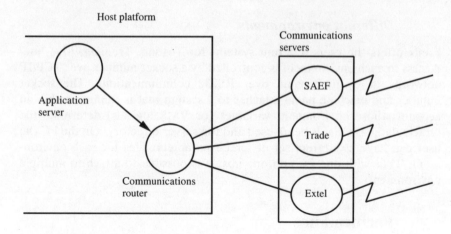

receives requests from other servers (via a C API), which routes the
request to the appropriate OS/2 communications engine (Figure 8.5).

Porting

We have kept the VAX as our development platform, as it provides an
excellent COBOL debugger, and we have adapted its Code Management
System for our particular requirements. Also, our first customers were
VAX sites.

The UNIX ports

Our first port to a UNIX platform was very painful. The architecture
ported across easily – but the ESQL had to use different datatypes to cater
for the way numbers were held. There was a lot of code to port – over a
thousand modules with copybooks that required datatypes to be modified
and move statements added.

Since that first experience, however, other UNIX ports have been
comparatively straightforward. The main differences are isolated within
the router, which requires a non-polling method of checking the state of
both TCP/IP sockets and internal pipes simultaneously. The main difficulties have been with the Oracle COBOL precompilers. The quality of
generated code varies from platform to platform, and, with the quantity
and variety of ESQL we have produced, we seem to find the bugs! So far,
we have ported to the following platforms:

Siemens	MX500 Sinix
Pyramid	OSx T Series
Pyramid	DCOSx S Series
Sun	SunOs

Sequent	DYNIX/ptx
Unisys	DYNIX/ptx
PS/2	SCO
RS/6000	AIX
HP	HPUX
DEC	OpenVMS Alpha

The CICS port

A large bank became interested in Synergo's settlement system, and liked the user interface, but they wanted it to run under CICS MVS. At that point we didn't see how it was possible to port this architecture to CICS, as Prefix was designed to run under operating systems that did not support transaction processing.

The bank was keen, and when we met its technicians it emerged that with some APPC communications development, and some rethinking about some of the core APIs, it began to look feasible to port the applications as they stood, and keep the user interface.

We supplied two communications solutions, and both are being used. The Networked DDE solution talks to an APPC gateway, which handles ASCII to EBCDIC conversions, and sends and receives normal Prefix messages. Each message interaction is a CICS transaction (Figure 8.6).

The second solution involved us writing an interface to IRMA Work-station for Windows, using their development kit. Then each PC can hold APPC conversations. This solution was for branches where there are only a

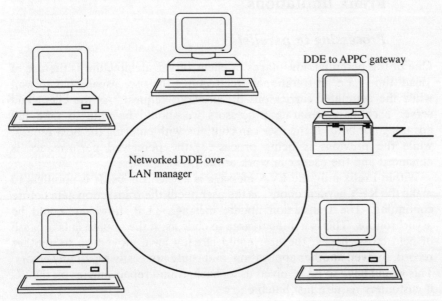

FIGURE 8.6
DDE TO APPC
GATEWAY.

DDE to APPC gateway

Networked DDE over
LAN manager

few PCs, and a network is not warranted. When porting to CICS the conversion of the APIs was comparatively painless. The major problem was that DB2 doesn't support many Oracle constructs, and a semi-automated, semi-handcrafted conversion of the ESQL proved time consuming. Also, the main method of producing reports under Oracle with VMS and UNIX is to spawn a new task to run SQL*PLUS reports. This is not possible under DB2, and we had to build COBOL servers.

Porting summary

In general, the porting of the architecture itself has been quite painless. This is due to the fact that the servers are context-free (otherwise each message could not be a separate CICS transaction, and we couldn't have done the CICS port), and that the messages are easily translated on any platform. Prefix is easy to port to different environments because there isn't much infrastructure code, and it uses ordinary operating system functionality. The main problems have been with the ESQL precompilers.

Originally, we were writing ESQL that we hoped could be easily ported to any RDBMS. It is now clear that the emerging standards agreement between RDBMS vendors for ESQL is a primitive lowest common denominator, and would involve much extra coding to implement. As most RDBMS suppliers support different versions of the higher-level functions and constructs, and different return codes, it would be a large undertaking to convert to a different database.

Prefix limitations

Processing in parallel

One of the potential advantages of client server architecture is the use of 'dead' time – i.e. in traditional architectures the user usually has to wait while the computer carries out the previous request. As the client and server each have separate processors we should be able to take full advantage of both. If the user can continue with entering the next request while the previous is being processed, the perceived performance is enhanced and the users can work at their own speed.

Within Prefix only the FVA message is asynchronous. It is pointless to make the KEY asynchronous, as the user needs the transaction data before continuing. The transaction update message TUP, however, could be asynchronous. This is a difficult area to code as, if the update fails because of field cross-checks, the user could already have moved on to another record, or even another application, and could not easily repair any errors. This would have to be resolved using background repair queues on the PC if customers require fast batch entry.

Local data

Currently, Prefix only has two sources of data against which to find values for a field – a local lookup table that is released once with the screens and a list satisfying user-supplied criteria, generated by a host server. It is often the case that the data and the selection criteria are unlikely to change during the day, so it makes sense to store this list on the PC, rather than fetch it again each time.

Availability

If the host should crash or communications are lost there is no facility to enter data locally on the PC. Rather than just stop work, it would be sensible to allow the input of transactions without host validation for sending later to the host.

Packet structure

We did not realize the importance of designing a highly flexible and extendible data packet. We built in some spare space, but were more concerned about complexity and length than flexibility. It is almost impossible to modify or extend the structure of the packet. There is no way of altering the basic structure while supporting live clients and sending out modifications and patches to servers. So we have had to overload heavily elements of the packet (i.e. make the same element take on different meanings in different contexts). We are limited by the packet structure, running out of usable bits to enhance the client/server interaction, or to build new data protocols.

Prefix futures

Field servers as well as application servers

Within an application all KEY, FVA and TUP messages are sent to one application server. It would make more sense to generalize this, so that field validation could be handled by specialist servers.

Object-oriented user interface

Currently, Prefix users have to choose what they want to do before they choose what to do it on. This is counter to current ideas of how systems should work. Selecting the object first, and then deciding what to do with it, is a much more powerful concept for users to grasp and is consistent with many Windows applications.

Distributed computing

Prefix as currently implemented doesn't allow servers to be on more than one platform. It is likely that we would provide such a facility by supplying the location of each server in a database table which would be sent to the PC when a new server was requested. The PC would become a dynamic name server, fed by database information.

The factors that have led to the success of Prefix as an architecture are:

- The client process runs from parameter files and so it is easy to build user interfaces.
- The client process is now DDE aware, so it is easy to build customized front-ends with tools such as Visual Basic.
- The server code is standardized, so it is comparatively simple to develop code generators. This standardization was made possible by mapping the user OLTP functions directly to server functions.
- The servers stay resident, so performance can be improved by loading data into memory at start-up time for later re-use, and Oracle SQL statements need be parsed only once.
- Context-free servers lead to robust code that was easy to maintain.
- Prefix is an open architecture – it has been comparatively easy to interface with other systems on-line, as we publish the message data structure and the rules to follow.

Prefix as middleware

When Prefix was first being developed the concepts of middleware were in their infancy. In order to produce a viable client/server architecture we produced, as part of Prefix, what are now known as middleware functions. These are

- A connection method between client and server process
- A message-passing mechanism with specified data formats and packing and unpacking functions
- Simple location transparency
- Sophisticated server management
- Application security and auditing, supplied as application servers.

Building OLTP architectures

From the experience of building Prefix, some general issues about OLTP architectures emerge:

- Even though it is possible to build in some simple middleware functionality, it would be advisable to use some networking middleware, such as DCE or APPN, to provide the networking facilities.
- The API between client and server should be an order of magnitude more general than the first requirements imply. You will always find a new way to use a client/server architecture.
- Try to make the infrastructure code small. Add functionality as add-on servers, not as extra core code. Then it is easier to modify these extra functions.
- Users query the database on OLTP systems, so ensure that the architecture also caters for enquiries with a reasonable response time. Consider using local data caches for enquiries on comparatively static data.
- Ensure that the user interface is easily modifiable. This is the most fashion-prone part of the system, and the users like to have their preferences.

9 Summary

The evolution of the style of computing known today as 'client/server' is an important milestone in computing history. It is a valuable way of conceiving, describing and building computer systems, which promises to liberate computing from the straightjacket of centralized designs.

Computers have promised much and delivered much less ever since their introduction into commercial life some thirty years ago for at least three reasons:

1. The early systems were just not powerful enough to do the things that business management really wanted to do.
2. They were applied to automate existing manual processes rather than to help companies to develop entirely new ways of working.
3. The productivity of programmers has never kept pace with the other developments in the industry, so that major applications typically took years to deliver.

With the advent of the powerful, affordable workstation, the advances in telecommunications and the increasingly open, market-driven nature of the computer industry, a number of great advances have been made on all these fronts. First, client and server platforms are much more powerful than before, and telecommunications bandwidth is freely available. We are increasingly limited more by our own imaginations and our willingness to change than we are by technology. Second, more and more examples are emerging of computers being applied to help companies run in a highly effective manner and in entirely new ways. The concept of 're-engineering' has taken hold and fundamentally changed some industries such as banking and insurance. Third, with the advent of powerful workstations, software tools have been developed which can eliminate the need for central application development altogether. End-users are increasingly able to develop new functions themselves in a few minutes that would have taken a central developer several weeks.

Describing systems in terms of 'clients', 'servers' and the links between seems a solid basis on which to build a real engineering approach to systems design and implementation. For too long, computer systems have been shrouded in mystique, but are now readily available for discussion and comprehension by non-specialists. This in turn means that they can come back under the control of business management, who have hitherto delegated control of IT to specialists.

Today, the most robust client/server systems – and those which deliver the best value for money – are those which provide access to existing data. Such systems also answer a frequent criticism of business management, namely that information that they need for decision making is not readily accessible. Meeting this need is a good way to start working with client/server systems.

There is an extensive range of products which combine to provide powerful facilities for interrogating relational databases. The selection of tools is one of the difficulties facing designers. The other important problem is the choice of style of system: to locate the 'business logic' exclusively on the workstation and communicate with SQL strings (PA~D), to locate the business logic on the server (P~AD) or to split the application logic (PA~AD). The first of these is the most robust and best served with international standards, but the last will probably prove to be the most effective in the long term.

Client/server systems have still to prove themselves capable of 'mission-critical' operation, and they have to solve the problems of managing large numbers of distributed computers. They have to blend the disciplines of mainframe operations with the flexibility of PCs. All of this will be achieved in time.

More importantly, the mechanisms for linking clients with servers must evolve and supporting standards must be agreed, so that workstations can be truly independent of their servers and enabled to connect freely to the services they require. This evolution is proceeding apace, with database vendors selling workstation tools, tool vendors selling connect mechanisms, transaction processing software vendors selling the benefits of independence, and operating system vendors trying to set *de facto* standards.

Client/server systems are not necessarily cheap nor are they pain-free. They imply significant change for the IT department and also for the users who must take more responsibility for their own systems. A business manager should expect to learn how to use a workstation and a range of software tools as part of his or her stock in trade. What we have tried to do in this book is to demystify the subject, to identify the current pitfalls, to point out the costs alongside the benefits, and to produce some examples of successful strategies.

Speculation

Gazing into the future is as dangerous as it is irresistible, especially in an industry as fast-moving as the IT industry. Some things are clear – in particular, the onward development of faster, cheaper, smaller technology will continue for some while. That means more powerful workstations, more powerful servers and more bandwidth both inside the computer and worldwide. Second, a new generation of children will grow up who take computers for granted and will be astonished to find commerce still riddled with manual processes. Third, our ability to process datatypes such as image and sound will improve, the workstation will be as capable of handling them as it is today of formatted text. This will also provide for such things as voice control of systems, freeing us from the tyranny of the keyboard and the mouse. This will lead us into a large range of products that we can only wonder at today.

Fourth, the range of services available to us from and on the workstation will grow. Such things as income tax returns would be far better handled as electronic objects than as paper forms. These services are likely to be supplied by specialist companies, both small and large, and therefore of high quality. Services that run on the workstation should be delivered as 'objects', if the OO community will only stop bickering about programming languages and get on with producing useful, packaged, interoperable objects, such as income tax handlers.

Much is currently written about the struggle between manufacturers and their pet standards for domination of the workstation, the network, the server. Will it be Windows NT or OS/2? Is UNIX dead? What is most likely is that there will be a small range of choices – as there is in most walks of life – with a few dominant products and a range of niche, specialist products. That being so, we can expect to see the emergence of standards and of products which will enable this range to work together productively. Important will be those which provide links between clients and their services and those which provide overall management.

Client/server systems are here to stay, although the term 'client/server' will probably evaporate, either because it is replaced by some new paradigm or because it becomes redundant: computer systems will be client/server by default. It remains to be seen how clients, servers and the mechanisms that link them evolve over the coming years.

Because they are more approachable by the ordinary mortal, they will unleash the power of computers more effectively over the next twenty years than has been the case over the last. We shall witness the ongoing computer revolution at first hand as old businesses are transformed, new businesses spring up and new facilities are provided to the home and to commerce and industry. It seems likely that it will bring as much opportunity and as much distress as has the motor car.

Appendix 1
LEGHAWK

The LEGHAWK notation emerged as the Client Server Working Group of the British Computer Society attempted to define the characteristics of client/server systems. The name LEGHAWK derives from the names of its seven members, five of whom are the authors of this book.

A client/server system is a computer system made up of discrete components each of which can request or provide definable services. We set ourselves the task of devising a notation capable of describing the measurable characteristics of these components, and their communication mechanisms. A standardized notation would have many advantages:

- It provides a mechanism for specifying the way components must interact.
- It allows comparisons of different client/server architectures.
- It helps communication between managers, users, sales people, analysts and technicians.

We wanted a notation that was accurate, concise, easily understood, and preferably not diagrammatic. It should be capable of supporting many levels of detail – the overall system design, the application level, the operational aspects and so forth.

Components

As discussed in earlier chapters, client/server systems have three major components, the presentation, the application, and the database, and these can be distributed across different platforms. Consider a simple LAN configuration such as in Figure A1.1.

This figure does convey a lot of information about the system, at a glance. However, there are very few accepted conventions about the symbols used, so the possibility for misunderstanding exists. Equally, in order to add more detail, there is little option but simply to add words all over the chart or to resort to a prose description.

Figure A1.1
Simple LAN
configuration.

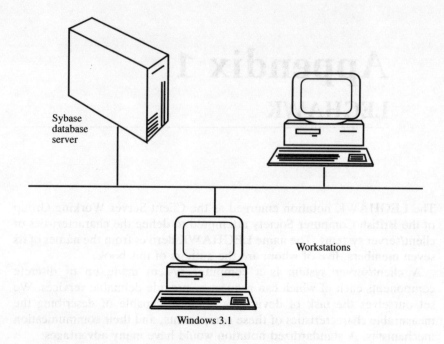

Sybase
database
server

Workstations

Windows 3.1

Such a system could be represented as

SYS = [PA] – [D]

which shows a system called SYS, where the P (presentation) and A (application, or business logic) reside on one platform, and the D (database) on another. The platform is represented by the brackets. This simple representation already shows an advantage over familiar diagrams such as the one above, as it is now clear on which platform the application is running.

The presentation and application components of SYS could be in the same program, or they could communicate in some way, with the application driving a presentation process. To indicate the extent to which P and A are entwined, we introduce some more notation

- PA indicates a single program with presentation and application code intermingled.
- P–A indicates a single program with presentation and application code in different modules, with a well-defined programming interface.P– –A indicates a loosely coupled presentation and application code which can easily be altered at run-time by changing, say, configuration files or dynamic libraries.
- P~~A indicates different programs which communicate.
- As ~~ indicates interprocess communication, we can rewrite as

SYS = [P− −A] ~~ [D].

The above discussion about P and A could also apply to other components, so AD could represent application logic tightly embedded in a database engine, such as stored procedures.

If SYS had many client platforms communicating with one database server, then

SYS = [P− −A] >~~ [D]

where the > symbol could be quantified.

SYS = [P− −A] 10>~~ [D]

could have about 10 client platforms. >~~ means communication of many to few, and <~~ means few to many. For example,

[P <~~ A]

could represent a presentation process interacting with many application processes on a single platform. There are six LEGHAWK components:

- *Presentation component P*. Presentation is concerned with interfacing to the outside world – either a user (via screen display, voice, keyboard, pointer, pen, etc.) or other computer systems (via alerts, timers, communication interrupts, etc.). Typically, in a GUI program, this controls the display of text or graphics and handles mouse and keyboard events, by writing to an API that controls the graphical environment.

- *Application component A*. The application component performs the user-defined business operation. Typically, this will decide on what appears on a screen, what are valid actions for a user to perform, validate user actions against business rules, perform any business logic and calculations, and access and update data.

- *Database component D*. The code performs the low-level routines required to access and reliably manage data on permanent storage. Usually this is done by a dedicated program, the database manager.

- *Routing component R*. The router is responsible for any intelligent control over the interprocess communication that may be required. A router may need to be aware of the data at an application level in order to route messages, and perhaps transform them to a different format. It accesses the APIs supplied by the communications component.

- *Communications component* ~C~. This provides the low-level inter-process communications within or between platforms.

- *Platform component [ ].* This is the hardware and its operating system software.

LEGHAWK was brought into being to improve our understanding of how any computer system works, not to rigidly define it. A large-scale component such as a database manager can in itself be described in terms of a Router, Communications, Application and Database code. This is not an indictment of the notation – part of the strength of LEGHAWK is that it can be applied at any required level of detail.

Many client/server architectures will have programs or processes that specialize in one or more of these components. For the purpose of clarity, it is not necessary to include those aspects of a program that are trivial or unimportant to the main operation of the system. For example, a program that specializes in routing may keep a log on hard disk or a database program may have a visual monitoring facility. Also, if there is a separate router task, then other programs will have some simple routing mechanism to communicate with it. Often a description of Communications will be adequate to describe the way the architecture handles interprocess communication, without the need for a Router component.

Attributes

Now that we have shown how to represent the way components are configured and interact we will describe in more detail how they behave. For example, the presentation interface could be one of a range of GUIs (Motif, MS-Windows, OS/2 PM, etc.) or character-based, character-based windows, Pen, 3270 screen, or even a file that is presented to another system. Under LEGHAWK, this attribute is given a name and a list of possible values:

'Presentation Interface' PresInt = Motif | MSWin | PM | Char | CharWin | Pen | 3270 | File.

The 'text in single quotes' is a free-format description of the attribute. Single quoted text can be used anywhere in LEGHAWK to add clarity to the notation. PresInt is the attribute name.

If an attribute requires a numeric value, such as

'Number of simultaneous user sessions' nUserSess = n

then the name will have a leading 'n'. Numeric values can have a single value (10), a minimum (>100), a maximum (<100) or a range (100–PL), where PL indicates the Physical Limitation of the platform or network.

The choice of which attributes to use in describing a system is, to a large extent, dependent on the audience. A base set should be used to ensure that all parties have a common understanding of the system, and then extra attributes can be added to cater for more specialist information. Some attributes could apply to all components (e.g. Vendor and LicenceFee).

In order to apply the attributes to the components we have uniquely to distinguish the components. This is done by subscripting the components and subsystems with either a letter of the alphabet or a meaningful name.

$$SYS_{site1} = [P- -A_{win}]_{pcw} \sim C_e \sim [D_{sy}]_{os2}$$

Note that we have introduced the $\sim C \sim$ symbol to indicate communications, as subscripting $\sim\sim$ is a typographical nonsense. The subscripts are chosen simply for ease of reference, in this case by their most important attribute, be it hardware type, operating system or even vendor.

If SYS represented a LAN implementation at the remote offices of a company, there could be a need for SYS to communicate with a central system:

$$SYS_{main} = SYS_{site1} \sim\sim [D]$$

Here SYS communicates with a central data server, as well as its own database. SYS_{site1} is now a sub-system of SYS_{main}. Sub-systems can be used in the notation as components, and encourage the modular approach to systems design. If there was another system SYS_{site2} also in use at some remote offices, then SYS_{main} could be made up of either sub-system:

$$SYS_{main} = (SYS_{site1} \mid SYS_{site2}) \sim\sim [D]$$

The I symbol means 'only one of', and II means 'at least one of'. So if SYS_{main} could support both SYS_{site1} and SYS_{site2} simultaneously,

$$SYS_{main} = (SYS_{site1} \parallel SYS_{site2}) \sim\sim [D]$$

In systems where parts of the application component are different programs, perhaps on different platforms, the responsibilities of each 'A' component must be defined:

'Application Responsibilities' AppResp =
    ScrDef II 'Defining the user screens'
    NavCtl II 'Controlling the way the user moves around the screen'
    DomChk II 'Ensuring entered values are of the correct type'
    BusVal II 'Ensuring that entered data is correct from a business point of view'
    DataAccess II 'Arranging for data access (builds and performs SQL)'

Or without the comments,

AppResp = ScrDef || NavCtl || DomChk || BusVal || DataAccess

Having defined the values of an attribute, system components can be described as a list of attributes with their values, for example,

$P--A_{win}$ = {PresInt = MSWin; nUserSess = PL; AppResp = ScrDef, NavCtl, DomChk, BusVal, DataAccess; MsgType = Sync; nSrv = 1; Lang = C};

where MsgType of Sync means that the user cannot send a new message until the previous one completes and nSrv of one means that there can be communication with only one database server at a time:

$\sim C_e\sim$ = {Cable = Ethernet; Proto = TCP; Mech = Sockets};

Some aspects of the example need not be expanded for many audiences. For example, [ ]$_{pcw}$ would be a PC running Windows. If it were relevant, the attributes of memory, disk space, speed, etc. could be spelt out to provide a requirements spec for the system. A salesperson may describe it as

[PA] – [D]

with attributes of price, flexibility, etc., whereas a systems integrator would be more concerned with platform and communications

$[PA]_{pcw} > \sim C_e\sim [D]_{os2}$

and a developer may be more concerned with the internals than the communications

$[P--A_{win}] - [D_{sy}]$

Prefix and LEGHAWK

As an example of how LEGHAWK can be applied to an existing client/ server system, we present the Prefix architecture, as described in the case study, in LEGHAWK notation. Prefix is made up of a number of possible sub-systems. In LEGHAWK this is expressed as

PFX 'Prefix architecture' =
$(PFX_{uv} \mid PFX_d \mid PFX_{mvs}) \sim C_{tcp}\sim PFX_{cs}$

PFX is made up of either the PFX_{uv} (UNIX or VMS system), the PFX_d (dumb terminal system), the PFX_{mvs} (CICS system) talking to a PFX communication server. Fleshing out the Unix subsystem:

PFX_u'Unix' =
$[P- -A_w >\sim C_{dde} \sim R_{atpc}]_{pc} >\sim C_{skt}\sim [R_{atu} \sim C_{fifo}\sim < A_{std} \sim C_{ora}\sim D_{ora}]_{unx}$

• $[P- -Aw > \sim C_{dde}\sim R_{atpc}]_{pc}$ The client sub-system. This is a PC running a number of copies of a Windows application loosely coupled with the presentation interface. There is a single router program that communicates within the PC via DDE.

• $[R_{atu} <\sim C_{fifo}\sim < A_{std} \sim C_{ora}\sim D_{ora}]_{unx}$ The server sub-system. A router communicates via a number of fifos, each of which can connect to a number of applications. The applications access an Oracle database using Oracle's own communication techniques.

Attributes of the components

• $P- -A_w$ = {nSess=PL; PresInt=MSWin; PresIPCProt=CutPaste, DDE; AppResp=ScrDef,NavCtl,DomChk; CltAPI=Msg; MsgType=A-sync; nSrv=1; Lang=ParamFile; }

The number of sessions is set by the machine limit. Windows provides the presentation interface. Cut & Paste and DDE are provided as part of the application. Screen definition, navigation and domain checking are provided as part of the client task. Communication is message based and asynchronous. Only one server can be accessed at a time. The application is driven by parameter files.

• C_{dde} = {Mech=DDE; MsgType=Async; nConn=PL; Proto= ShMem}

• R_{atpc} = {ProtoConv=(DDE,(Skt | RS232)); MsgType=Async; nConn=PL}

The PC router converts DDE messages into sockets or RS232 communications. Messages are asynchronous, and the number of connections is limited only by the machine.

• C_{skt} = {Mech=Skt; Proto=TCP; Cable=Ethernet; MsgType= Async; nConn=PL}

- R_{atu} = {ProtoConv=(Fifos,(Skt|RS232)); MsgType=Async; nConn <=25}

The UNIX router converts protocol between fifos and either sockets or rs232. The messages are asynchronous, and there is a maximum of 25 connections per Router.

- C_{fifo} = {Mech=Fifo; MsgType=Async; nConn=PL;}
nConn=PL indicates that a number of connections can be established over one fifo.

- Astd = {Life=SCFG; Lang=C,Cobol; nThr=1; nInst=SCFG; nCtxtArea=0; CltAPI=Msg; AppResp=BusVal,DataAcess; AppLock =SoftLock;}

An application's duration is statically configurable. It can be written in C or COBOL, is single threading, but the number of instances is also configurable. The applications are context-free, and use a message API. The application is responsible for business logic and data access. Data is locked at application level by a soft-locking mechanism.

- D_{ora}= {DataPres=SQL; ConCurr=Pess; UpdGran=Row; SecRes =Table; Lock=Row}

The Oracle database presents data as SQL, uses a pessimistic concurrency algorithm, has row-level update and locking, and restricts access by table.

As we said at the beginning of this appendix, we wanted a notation that was accurate, concise, easily understood, and preferably not diagrammatic. It should be capable of supporting many levels of detail – the overall system design, the application level, the operational aspects, etc. We feel that the LEGHAWK notation meets these requirements, and has been used to describe quite complex systems. Like most notations, it takes a little time and practice to become fluent and confident.

It has been suggested that some automation of LEGHAWK would be possible to provide a mechanical means of checking systems for completeness. Whether such developments occur or not, only time will tell. Whatever LEGHAWK's fate, the design of computer systems could certainly do with more formality and discipline.

Appendix 2
Transaction processing systems

Transactions have existed almost as long as humans have inhabited the earth. Everyone has been in the situation where somebody else has something you want and you have something to give in return. This is normally goods in return for cash, but as we move forward into the cashless society these transactions have moved to computers and transaction processing systems to look after them. The concept of a transaction is well understood, that after a negotiation the transaction is completed (committed), or both sides reset (backout) and each partner returns to the state that they were in before the negotiation started. Quite often a receipt may be handed out to the buyer (confirmation message) and a till roll will be updated on the seller's side (journal).

There is little difference with computer systems, in fact, they sometimes use the same words in the paragraph above as the commands to a transaction processing systems. They also take the concept much further; not only is there just one customer but also there are multiple suppliers and they are all at different stages of the process at any point in time. Let us consider some cases, each becoming more complicated and by the end you will see why transaction systems have used about 50% of traditional computer power for the last 25 years, and will do so for the next ten or more years.

The simplest example can be illustrated by considering a person buying tomatoes at a market stall. There are various stages in this simple transaction:

1. The buyer looks at the stall to see if there are tomatoes and of the right quantity and quality and works out the cost.
2. The buyer checks to see if he has enough money to pay for the tomatoes.
3. The buyer makes his order and hands over the correct cash.
4. The seller places the money in the till and automatically logs the transaction on a till roll.
5. The seller hands over the tomatoes.
6. The buyer walks off.

This simplistic example illustrates some key points:

1. An inquiry was performed.
2. A request for services was made.
3. A log record was made.
4. The service was performed.
5. The transaction completed.

A basic transaction processing systems is no different, the application performs the specific business stages, and the transaction system looks after the logging and recovery aspect.

Consider the unfortunate case where a car mounts the pavement and knocks down the seller. There are really two cases here:

1. After the shock, the buyer has not got the tomatoes and wants his or her money back, so the transaction is backed out and the money returned; or
2. The seller is knocked out for a few minutes, and when the seller comes to, looks for a till receipt. If one exists, the seller puts the tomatoes back on the stall and hands back the cash, if he has any in his hand.

In computing terms, the first case is known as Rollback or Dynamic Transaction Backout (DTB), and the second as Emergency Restart. This level of recovery/restart required in the example above could be implemented by the application programmer in every transaction that is written, but this would be extremely expensive, so like all computing systems, common functions are encapsulated together to reduce the effort, and thereby the cost to the business of the application programmer creating the business solution. The simple case above could be implemented using a database with the recovery features defined above. It is when the solution requires many sellers, many buyers all processing at the same time where some of the transactions may have simultaneous multiple sellers, and to add to it may have gone to lunch in the middle of the transaction that a transaction processor is needed. So at this point we can define a transaction processing system to be one that allows the running of multiple transactions at the same time with an inbuilt data-locking system, integrity, priority, security interfaces, recovery/restart, some management functions to allow the operators/managers of the system to understand what is happening in the system.

Some transaction processing systems have historically grown out of teleprocessing monitors. Probably the best known of these is IBM's Customer Information Control System (CICS) known over most of the world as 'Kicks'. Others have been specifically built to perform transaction processing (for example, Tandem Non-Stop Systems and Stratus Systems). The teleprocessing monitor itself came into being to improve application programmer productivity by giving a higher-level Application Programming Interface to the inbuilt system communications component, along

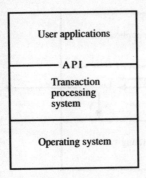

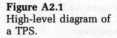

Figure A2.1
High-level diagram of
a TPS.

with some integrated connectivity and restart/recovery functions. The transactional capabilities were added in parallel as higher-level functionality was added to the data access methods.

It was also understood at that time and the economics have not changed, the Chinese rule of users: 'If it costs *x* to write a system for one user, it will cost ten times that for two and a hundred times for three or more.' It is here that the real payback comes from using a transaction processing system, the application programmer can write his or her business application with little knowledge of what else is going on in the system, so the costs are equivalently reduced.

Some of the discrete components diagrammed in Figure A2.1 may be subsumed into larger components depending upon the actual implementation. In the totally degenerate case, where the application environment of the system contains the transaction processing primitives, the user application will interface straight to the operating system without all the visible layers shown in Figure A2.1.

Most transaction systems have an application programming interface which provides transaction services, for example:

1.   Begin transaction
2.   Commit protected resources
3.   Rollback protected resources

Probably the greatest number of systems using this technology is Novell transaction servers built round the keyed access BTRIEVE technology, though the greatest number of people who depend on transaction processing systems use IBM CICS.

Transaction processing systems started to implement distribution technologies more than fifteen years ago, the first of these being transparent data access – in LEGHAWK notation, [P–A] >~C~[D]. The function invoked found that the resource referred to was not local, by interrogating some sort of resource repository, and if so, packaged this request for access to the resource in an 'envelope' and forwarded it to the system address named in the repository. On arrival, the receiving agent unpacked the

Figure A2.2
Local and remote
resources.

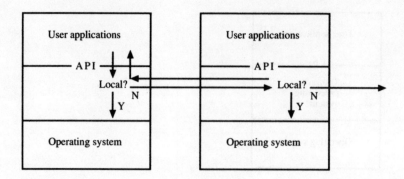

request and issued it as if it were a local request . If successful, the answer
was then repackaged in another 'envelope' to be returned to the requesting
system, where it was unwrapped and presented back to the requester
transparently. Here the two systems were functionally equivalent.
Included in this function was the case where the second system's repository
stated that the named resource was remote, so the same procedure as
before was invoked. Obviously, checks were made to see that the looping
situation was diagnosed, e.g. resource A on system A was defined on
system B and vice versa on system B. So a simple diagram of the action is
as shown in Figure A2.2.

A transaction processing system provides sets of services beneath its API
to lessen the amount of work that application programmers have to write.
Applications may be written in a variety of third- and fourth-generation
languages. COBOL is still the prevalent language in the TPS world, though
C is gaining a little ground, especially in the UNIX and OS/2 sphere. A
variety of platforms also support PL/I.

The normal way to create an executable module to run in transaction
processing systems is to input the source program into the TPS translator
which scans the source for a trigger, (e.g. EXEC CICS) and creates
language-dependent calls. The output is then input to the compiler and
linker to create the executable module. This same technique was employed
for the EXEC SQL relational language some years after its introduction in
transaction processing systems. A high-level schematic of a transaction
processing system could be shown as Figure A2.3.

Most resources that are used by a transaction processing systems
application have an associated resource definition entry associated with
them that contains the specifics of that resource, so simplistically a keyed
file will have a file entry, a terminal, a terminal entry, and so on.

As an example, the user transaction issues a READ. Control is
transferred to file control, which accesses the relevant resource entry in the
file resource definition which has been configured to say that the file is
remote, the request is packaged up and the remote system accessed with a
separate transaction, known, for example, in CICS as the mirror. As its

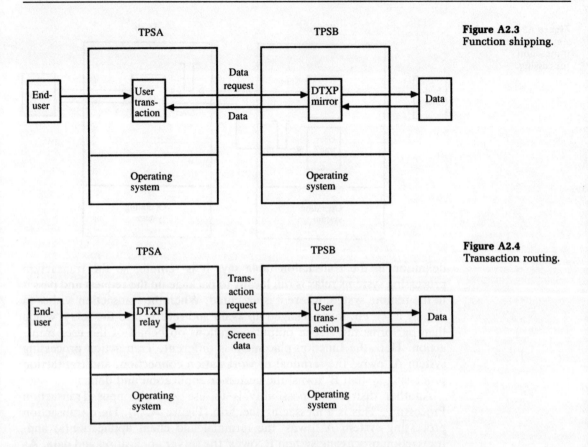

Figure A2.3
Function shipping.

Figure A2.4
Transaction routing.

name suggests, this mirrors the original request, a READ in this case. The function is performed and the resultant data is packaged up and returned to the invoking system. File control then removes the envelope and passes the data back to the invoking application transparently to the application programmer.

This scenario can be extended to recoverable resources, such that if the command was to do a READ UPDATE, the mirror would remain holding the locks on the updated data until a SYNCPOINT was issued either explicitly or implicitly by the invoking transaction and the mirror will, on the syncpoint flow, either commit or backout the update. So in this simple case, it can be seen that transaction processing system A 'owns' the stimulus that started the transaction the application and the commit scope; and transaction processing system B 'owns' the data. This example can be expanded to transaction processing system A having local data as well. Also, there can be more than one remote transaction processing system attached to a transaction.

The next distribution technology is transaction routing (Figure A2.4). Here the end-user invokes a screen transaction, the local resource

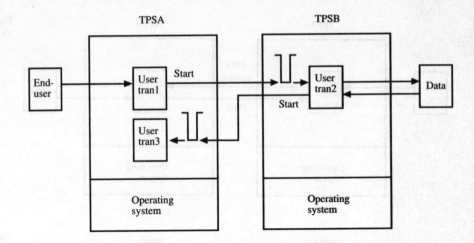

definition in the transaction table says it is remote, so the transaction processing systems relay is run locally to package up the request and pass it to the remote system where it is executed. When the transaction wishes to display a screen, it is packaged up again and returned to the relay, which then performs the screen output operations on behalf of the user transaction. Here the function placement is different. Transaction processing system A 'owns' the terminal or workstation connection, and transaction processing system B 'owns' the customer application and data.

Another distributed possibility is to use Asynchronous Transaction Processing. This is a messaging scenario (Figure A2.5). Here transaction processing system A 'owns' the terminal and client application(s) and, transaction processing system B 'owns' the server application and data. As opposed to the synchronous examples of function shipping above, communication is asynchronous. This leads to a different design, since each of the three transactions that run in the system run as separate units of work.

Remote procedure call is a recent addition to distribution in a transaction processing system environment. Again the attributes of transparent remote data access are added to the LINK/CALL mechanisms. This allows distributed programs to run within a logical unit of work without having to write explicit communications code (Figure A2.6). This is the transaction processing system equivalent of a remote procedure call. Here transaction processing system A 'owns' the end-user and the client application, and transaction processing system B 'owns' the server application and data. All communication is masked by the LINK/RETURN mechanisms of TPS, and the same considerations that apply to function shipping also apply here. CICS has coined the phrase Distributed Program Link for the function.

The final distributed technology that is built into transaction processing systems is DTP (Distributed Transaction Processing, not Desk Top Publishing!). This capability performs the same function as Distributed Program Link but at a lower level. From Figure A2.7 it can be seen that the

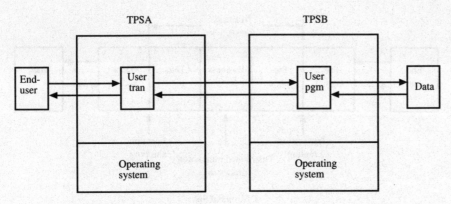

Figure A2.6
Distributed program link.

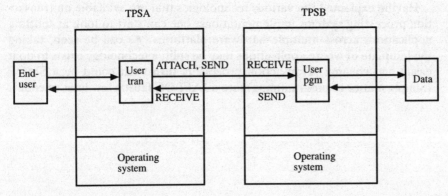

Figure A2.7
Application to application.

interface between the application and application is at a SEND/RECEIVE level. This has pluses and minuses. The plus is that the programmer can optimize the flows and has the ability, if the application allows it, to have the applications running at both ends of the communications link at the same time, thus shortening the total response time. Also on some implementations the programmer is responsible for Syncpointing the data at the end of a transaction. The minus side of this is that the application programmer needs to understand the APPC protocols that transport the data between these two or more consenting applications.

Transaction processing systems normally use the underlying communications products to implement layer 5 functions such as APPC, which, for example, include Virtual Telecommunications Access Method (VTAM) on the IBM ES mainframes, ENCINA on AIX or HP UNIX, or Extended Services on IBM OS/2. Also specific implementations can have additional communication with other transaction processing systems on the same platform with protocols that are specific to that platform (e.g. NetBIOS on OS/2 and TCP/IP on UNIX and OS/2) (Figure A2.7).

Figure A2.8
Combining it
together.

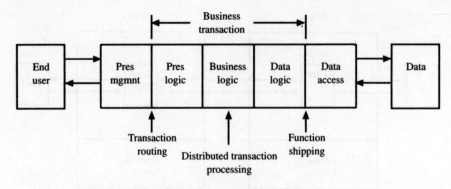

Having explained the various technologies that are available on transaction processing systems implementations, one can start to look at splitting applications across multiple hardware platforms. As can be seen, taking the template of where applications may be split, a technology exists to do it easily and cheaply. Transaction processors turn what could be a SMOP (Simple matter of programming) into a JAFLOC (Just a few lines of code).

Glossary

3270 IBM terminal family, widely used in large-scale IBM transaction processing systems.

ACID The desirable properties of a transaction: atomicity, consistency, isolation, durability.

API Application Programming Interface – the procedures through which a programme communicates with other (usually software) products.

APPC Advanced Program-to-Program Communications. An application-to-application session mechanism built on **LU6.2** (*qv*). Invented by IBM.

Application component (A) The functional or business logic of an application, excluding the presentation, data and communications functions.

Application system A process or collection of processes to carry out some user-defined purpose.

ASCII American Standard Coded Information Interchange Standard for mapping character data into binary notation. Used on PCs and derivatives.

BCS The British Computer Society.

Cap-sizing The result of too much right-sizing.

CBI Character Based Interface. Contrast with **GUI** (*qv*).

CICS Customer Information Control System. IBM's premier transaction processing system, now being ported to a variety of platforms.

Client (noun) A requester of services. May be hardware or software.

Client (adj) Having the attributes of a client.

Client/server architecture The external description of a computer system which identifies **clients**, **servers** (*qv*) and the interfaces between them. Can be multi-level; a client or server at one level could be made of up both clients and servers at a lower level.

Communications component (~C~) The linkage between a client and a server. If no detail is required in the description, this may be replaced in LEGHAWK notation by a single '~'.

CORBA Common Object Request Broking Architecture. A standard approach for passing messages from one object to another across platforms.

131

CSG   The Client/Server Group – a sub-set of the BCS.

Database component (D)   A structured collection of user data, including the data management software and storage hardware. It is possible to represent databases hierarchically – something seen as a single database at one level may be broken down into a number of databases at a lower level.

DBA   DataBase Administrator. The person or department responsible for the design and running of a database.

DBMS   Database management system. The system software which manages a database.

DCE   Distributed Computing Environment. A standard way of linking computer systems together in a seamless fashion. Likely to be implemented on both proprietary and open computer systems.

DDE   Dynamic Data Interchange. A mechanism to allow software objects to exchange data in a Microsoft Windows environment.

Distributed   Split across more than one node. May be data or process or both.

Down-sizing   A term coined by consultants to improve their cash flow. Describes the replacement of large, expensive, proprietary mainframes by small, cheap, open systems.

EBCDIC   Extended Binary Coded Data Interchange C IBM's 8-bit extension to BCD, the earlier standard for mapping character data into binary notation. Used on mainframes.

EIS   Executive Information System. System designed to deliver information in a form that Executives will find acceptable. Senior version of MIS.

Ethernet   A physical protocol and cable type used for LANs. An international standard.

GUI   Graphical user interface, usually with mouse, windows, icons, etc.

Heritage system   An existing system you'd like to hang on to. See **Legacy system**.

ISV   Independent Software Vendor. A producer of software who is not controlled by hardware vendors.

LAN   Local area network. Telecommunications mechanism originally confined within a building, but increasingly extending around the world.

Left-sizing   The management of whatever is left, after down-sizing and right-sizing.

Legacy system   An existing system you've been left with. See **Heritage system**.

LEGHAWK   A notation for describing client/server architectures, devised by the BCS Client Server group working party. The name is made from the initial letters of their surnames.

Link/channel   A means of passing messages.

LU6.2   SNA subset used for **APPC** (*qv*) communications.

MB and Mb   Megabyte and megabit respectively.

Message   Data or events (such as requests or responses/replies) passed over a communications link/channel.

Middleware   A term loosely covering a range of services such as message-passing and transaction handling, provided by a layer of software between the operating system and the application.

MPE   Hewlett Packard's proprietary operating system.

MTBF   Mean Time Between Failures: a measure of reliability.

MTTR   Mean Time To Repair: a measure of the 'repairability' of a product, the responsiveness of the service organization, the capability of the service organization or a blend of all three.

MVS   IBM's proprietary operating system for its large 'mainframe' systems. Includes MVS/ESA, MVS/SP, etc.

Network1. Two or more hosts/nodes connected by (physical) communications links/channels. 2. A collection of software and hardware allowing two or more nodes to communicate.

NFS   Networked File System. Mechanism for accessing files on a remote platform, as if they were local.

Node   A computer system treated as a single point in a network. Physically a single (hardware) computer system; logically might be a network in its own right.

NT   An abbreviation for Windows NT, Microsoft's operating system for the workstation and LAN server.

OLE   Object Linking Environment. A mechanism to allow software objects to communicate in a Microsoft Windows environment.

OLTP   On-Line Transaction Processing. The transactions are often envisaged as low in complexity, high in volume, and likely to update a database.

OS   Operating System. The layer of software which drives the underlying hardware and provides services to higher layers of software.

OS/2   IBM's operating system for the workstation and LAN server.

Platform   The Hardware and System Software on which an application system runs.

Presentation component (P)   The part of a system which controls how the system appears to the user. It may be a GUI or CBI, in the case of presentation to human users. It may be a series of voltages in the case of presentation to a machine.

Process   A strict sequence of operations (carried out by some processor which could be human or non-human, i.e. a CPU). It is possible to represent processes hierarchically – something seen as a process at one level may be broken down into a number of (sub-)processes at a lower level.

RAID   Redundant Array of Inexpensive Disks. A way of providing high levels of reliability by linking disk drives to form arrays, capable of withstanding the loss of one of the drives. Different linkage methods are used in RAID 1, 2, 3, 4 and 5 configurations.

Request   A message from a client requiring a service to a server (or servers) which provides the service. A **response/reply** may or may not be expected.

Response/reply   A message from a server to a client which has previously sent a request to the server. May be what the client asked for or some indication of why it cannot be supplied.

Right-sizing   A term coined by consultants to maintain the cash flow generated by **Down-sizing**. Describes the more sensible exploitation of small, cheap, open systems to handle tasks more cost/effectively than mainframes.

Router component (R)   Directs a message to the appropriate client or server, usually over a network.

RPC   Remote Procedure Call. An interface allowing one software component to pass control to another, even across communication links. A standard RPC is part of DCE.

Server   Provides a service to one or more clients (receives a request and returns some response). Can be noun/entity or adjective/attribute (e.g. server process). Can be hardware or software.

Service   Anything carried out by a server on request from a client resulting in a response (e.g. carry out function, transfer data).

SNA   Systems Network Architecture. IBM's published but proprietary communications architecture.

Sockets   An application-to-application session mechanism, built on TCP/IP.

SQL   Structured Query Language. Invented by IBM for manipulating relational databases. Now an international standard and widely implemented.

System   A collection of hardware, software and communications links to carry out a (user-defined) objective.

System software   Software such as the operating system, which together with **Hardware** makes up the platform. Usually supplied by a software vendor.

TCP/IP   A commonly used transport mechanism. A *de facto* international standard.

TLA   Three-letter acronym.

Token ring   A physical protocol and cable type used for LANs, developed and promoted by IBM. An international standard.

TOP END   AT&T's new middleware package which provides distributed transaction management and robust message passing.

TPC   Transaction Processing Council. An independent body set up to provide comparative performance figures for a variety of platforms running a variety of workloads.

tps   transaction per second.

TPS   Transaction Processing System.

UNIX   An operating system developed by AT&T Bell Labs for easy migration to new hardware platforms. Increasingly used in commercial environments.

VMS   DEC's proprietary operating system.

VTAM   Virtual Telecommunications Access Method. IBM's software package for handling telecommunications.

WAN   Wide area network. Originally a telecommunications mechanism covering large geographical distances. Increasingly difficult to separate from **LANs** (*qv*).

XA   International standard interface defining how transactions should be defined and manipulated.

Registered trade names

Trademarks mentioned in the text include: TPC - Transaction Processing Council; IBM (APPC, CICS, SNA, PS/2, AIX, Encina, OS/2); AT&T (TOP END); Microsoft (Pentium, OLE?, DDE?, Windows, Windows NT); UNIX (X-Windows?); Apple Macintosh; DEC; (VMS, VT100); ISO; Novell; OSF; X-Open; Hewlett Packard (HP); Sybase; Synergo (Prefix); nCUBE; Sun (SunOS); Siemens (MX500 Sinix); Pyramid (OSx T, DCOSx S).

Index